EMPOWERING
THE AMERICAN CONSUMER

EMPOWERING THE AMERICAN CONSUMER

Corporate Responsiveness and Market Profitability

A. Coskun Samli

Q

QUORUM BOOKS
Westport, Connecticut • London

Library of Congress Cataloging-in-Publication Data

Samli, A. Coskun.
   Empowering the American consumer : corporate responsiveness and market
profitability / A. Coskun Samli.
     p. cm.
   Includes bibliographical references and index.
   ISBN 1–56720–378–7 (alk. paper)
   1. Consumers—United States. 2. Consumer protection—United States. 3.
Corporations—United States. 4. United States—Economic conditions. I. Title.
HC110.C6 S26 2001
381.3—dc21   00–032817

British Library Cataloguing in Publication Data is available.

Library of Congress Catalog Card Number: 00–032817
ISBN: 1–56720–378–7

First published in 2001

Quorum Books, 88 Post Road West, Westport, CT 06881
An imprint of Greenwood Publishing Group, Inc.
www.quorumbooks.com

Printed in the United States of America

The paper used in this book complies with the
Permanent Paper Standard issued by the National
Information Standards Organization (Z39.48–1984).

10 9 8 7 6 5 4 3 2 1

This book is dedicated to businesspeople who believe
in making money by treating consumers kindly and gently.

Contents

Contents

Preface

Some years ago in the preface of one of my earlier books I stated: "It is my hope that this controversial book will raise many issues and be instrumental in the emergence of numerous decisions, debates and above all, socially responsible marketing decisions that will benefit society as a whole" (Samli 1992). It is totally the same sentiment in which the present book is written. Only the stakes are higher and the issues are more far-reaching.

Although business decisions are made at the micro level, they have very critical macro implications. The market capitalism is here but where it goes from here is perhaps the most important consideration that would touch us all. The connection between these macro and micro implications touches our lives constantly. Thus, the micro decisions must be just right so that the macro conditions in our economy would improve.

Certainly we know that the market is not perfect. But should it get worse? Should we not have a say as to where it may go? Could the market really correct itself if there was no government? What happens if it is allowed to go in the direction of self-destruction like it almost did in the Great Depression of early 1930s? It is maintained here that unless conscious and proactive actions take place to benefit the corporate entity and consumers simultaneously, the decisions and behavior of certain individual firms could be detrimental to the whole society because they have too much power and

Exhibit P-1
Contribution of Empowering the Consumer

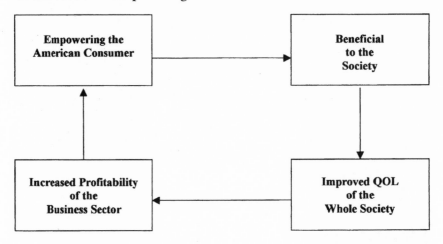

they don't concern themselves with consumer well-being. In essence they are driven by *greed* rather than *reason* and *concern*.

This book takes the position that the market system, in general, functions like a double-entry accounting process. If consumer value as a whole is enhanced the corporate profit picture also enhances, and this takes society to a higher economic plateau. So why this book? Because although on the surface, at the writing of this book in late 1999 and early 2000 the American economy is doing quite well, in reality it is quite derailed. And if it continues in the same way, there may be a disaster. Many very powerful firms are so much in search of their own advantages over their competitors, they almost forget that they owe their very existence to consumers. Instead of generating consumer value they are engaged in what seems to be an endless merger mania. They are gaining more and more power by buying out their competition and are becoming so powerful that they are terrorizing the consumer. We must go back to having powerful consumers who articulate their needs and wishes. The fulfillment of these needs and wishes lifts up the economy to higher plateaus. In other words the most important ingredient of a nation's economy is its *people*. Given a chance, they all strive to improve themselves and their lives, but in the process they improve the economy as well.

The general theme of this book is illustrated in Exhibit P-1, which shows that empowering the American consumer will benefit society as a whole. It will expand the economy, make it more equitable and improve the quality of life (QOL) for all. This situation will improve the profit picture of the corporate entity simultaneously. The exhibit makes a very critical point that the corporate entity is very responsible in the empowerment of the American consumer. It has the power and it is the responsibility to improve its own profit picture the right way and start an upward economic spiral for us all.

Market capitalism works best when consumers are powerful enough to make choices to exercise their prerogatives and make the best possible decisions for themselves. However, they must be tooled up for this all-inclusive activity. That is why empowering the consumer is critical. However, from a business perspective, as consumers are empowered the company's profitability will also be increased, thus the whole society will be better off.

The book begins with a brief introduction that articulates the two extreme views about the market. It proposes that the market is not sacrosanct and if left alone, it does not function in an all-beneficial and corrective manner. It can easily be derailed.

Chapter 1 sets the tone of the book by first discussing the extraordinary accumulation of economic power and how it is reducing competition in favor of increasing market power by merger mania. It warns about emerging oligopolies and the damage they could cause by limiting competition.

Chapter 2 explores the plight of the American consumer. It suggests that the middle class is slowly eroding and American society is taking a bipolarized posture. Creating a very large group of poor people and a small group of extremely rich people and allowing an ever-growing gap between these two groups is not at all good for the future of the American economy.

Chapter 3 examines what idealistically is called the equal opportunity consumer. It looks into those consumers who are considered frail. And it proposes that consumer frailty is self-perpetuating. Again if left alone things are not getting any better.

Chapter 4 establishes the fact that complexity begets more complexity. While it may be useful to those who can take advantage of it, for a large majority of the populace, increasing complexity in society is creating hardship.

Chapter 5 deals with the magnificent American economy. First, the tremendous capacity, potential and opportunities that exist in the American market are discussed. Then conditions surrounding the imminent deterioration in the American economy are examined.

Chapter 6 looks at the very political issue of the federal government versus states' rights. Although much pressure is exerted to achieve more states' rights, the chapter advocates that if each state is left alone to maximize whatever it is performing, the country as a whole would suboptimize.

Chapter 7 explores another controversial and political issue, deregulation. It posits that all deregulation activities are not necessarily good. It maintains, therefore, that in some cases regulation rather than deregulation is necessary to accelerate competitive activity.

Chapter 8 discusses what the American economy is, a mixed economy. Here the private and public sectors should work together to not allow excessive business failures. They should bear the cost of creating equal opportunity, and they should see to it that there will be an optimal balance between the private and public sectors.

Chapter 9 looks into how growth strategies can be implemented and the economy can grow faster. It posits that there are government-initiated macro growth strategies that will further accelerate the private sector's micro growth strategies.

Chapter 10 gets into a highly sensitive area, education. It points out that unless people are given equal opportunity to receive good education and training, the American consumer cannot be empowered. The human resources of our society must be fully developed.

Chapter 11 analyzes the environment and the infrastructure. It posits that environmental deterioration and infrastructure development, or lack thereof, are somewhat related. It is essential that we optimize the conditions for the private sector to flourish. Hence, the infrastructure must be optimalized for the growth of the private sector.

Chapter 12 examines a very critical area of generating consumer value. This is accomplished by value marketing. Different criteria are examined as to how companies can further create consumer value through value marketing.

Chapter 13 pulls the whole book together and reinforces the need of and the mechanics for empowering the American consumer. It also suggests some key research areas that are critical for the future of the American economy.

REFERENCE

Samli, A. Coskun (1992). *Social Responsibility in Marketing*. Westport, CT: Quorum Books.

Acknowledgments

Many people have contributed directly and indirectly to the development of this book. Early on, my thinking was formed by some of the outstanding professors I had the privilege to work with at Michigan State University. Two of these names particularly stand out, Frank Childs and Abba Lerner. These two gentlemen had much to say, and I had much to learn.

My friend, colleague and coauthor of many years, Professor Joe Sirgy of Virginia Tech, always has been available to argue, interact, discuss and sometimes disagree. His influence on my thinking has been profound. Because of him I learned to question my statements and be more to the point.

My colleagues at the University of North Florida knowingly or unknowingly have been pulled into many discussions pertaining to various points of this book. Dr. Bruce Kavan, by working on different articles with me and, in the process, by exchanging ideas, was very helpful. Dr. Bruce Fortado, by being around next to my office and interacting with me much of the time, helped me formulate some of my thinking. Dr. Adel El-Ansary always has been a source of inspiration and ideas. Dr. Ronald Adams with his wit and wisdom always questioned my comments and statements. That always is stimulating. My dean, Earle Traynham, and my department head, Robert Pickhardt, were kind enough to give me support and encouragement so that I could produce this volume just as I did the previous volumes. Dr. Roger

Dickinson of the University of Texas at Arlington directed my attention to many important references. He encouraged me through his cynicism.

This book could not have been written without the research help I received from my two graduate assistants. First, Tomas Jedlik, now a consultant with McKenzie and Co., started the basic support materials based on my needs expressed in the outlines I gave him. He had developed his research skills to the point that I had outstanding support for all the chapters in this book. Then, my current assistant, Nebine Chhay, has managed to give me calculations, additional materials, and a sounding board for many of my ideas.

Our secretaries Kimberly Anderson, Annette Driscoll, Susan Watts and Shenika Jefferson were always there to help. Without them, I could not function.

Hundreds of my graduate students listened, reacted, argued and sometimes disagreed with me about many points that are made in this book. They were patient enough to listen to my, at times, rather-out-of-the-ordinary ideas. I owe them much. Beverly Chapman gave me a helping hand in editing this book. As usual she did a great job. Finally, Bea Goldsmith read, argued and redirected me on many parts of this book. Her contributions are quite visible in some parts of this volume.

To these and many others who, over the years, discussed, interacted or researched these issues with me, I extend my deep gratitude. This is an unusual and a controversial book. I certainly hope that it will generate much-needed healthy discussion and will make a difference. However, I am solely responsible for its contents. I certainly hope that it makes a modest but noticeable contribution to the well-being of all of my fellow Americans without leaving anybody behind.

Introduction

MARY MARY QUITE CONTRARY, HOW DOES YOUR ECONOMY GROW?

Your economy grows not by derailing the current American markets, not by discriminating against the consumers, not by allowing anarchy in the economy and not at all by being inactive in sociopolitical and economic arenas.

Mary, your economy will grow if consumers are empowered. If people are given equal opportunity to choose, to advance, to work and to accomplish; if competition in the economy is not undermined, if economic power is not allowed to concentrate in a few hands indiscriminately, your economy will certainly grow.

In an important book Lester Thurow (1996) discussed the future of American capitalism. He posited that capitalism is not likely to implode as communism and other earlier economic systems did. Capitalism does not have viable competitors, so if consumers are disappointed with the treatment they receive from capitalism, they will not be able to rush to another system. However, Thurow claimed that capitalism is not likely to self-destruct nor is it likely that it will collapse. But *stagnation* is a real danger. Stagnation here is related to declining competition. Moore (1996) pointed out that American competition is not what it used to be. It is changing in such a way that it is almost unrecognizable. Indeed, it is difficult to see if the way American competition is changing will be better for the American consumer. If the American consumer were to have a better quality of life and if American markets were to make progress, which they are so capable of doing, American competition must be enhanced, not changed drastically or allowed to deteriorate, and above all the American consumer must be empowered.

Empowerment, according to Blanchard, Carlos and Randolph (1996), is not just giving power to people. It is releasing the knowledge, experience and motivation that people already have. However, this definition does not go far enough. Empowerment should also mean making sure that people have equal opportunity to participate in this released knowledge, experience and motivation. This book in this and its subsequent chapters attempts to explore how the American consumer can be empowered so that the American society can reach a higher economic plateau.

THE ROLE OF THE ECONOMIC SYSTEM

It does not matter if it is communism, nazism, socialism or capitalism, the reason for existence of any economic-political system is to provide the populace with the best possible level of economic well-being so that they can have better than just a tolerable quality of life. This better-than-tolerable quality of life is related to how much freedom of choice consumers have, and how much consumer education, consumer protection and consumer information exist in society. In other words, consumers must have access to the freedom of choice, which is primarily dependent on the level of competition in the economy. If the economy does not display an adequate level of competition, business and government sectors are not pressured into providing consumer education, consumer protection and consumer information. These are necessities of consumer empowerment.

Competition is the essence of consumer empowerment (Davis 1975). It facilitates consumer information, consumer protection and consumer education along with consumer choice and consumer opportunities to advance economically. These, in turn, make it possible for the economic quality of life in the society to advance.

Despite all the mass media hype at the time of writing of this book, the American economy is not doing nearly as well as it could. It is necessary to look at it more critically. For instance: at this point in time unemployment figures are the lowest they have been in two decades, but no one asks: are these people all working full time (40 hours a week or more) or less than full time? Are they receiving reasonable pay? What about those who have given up and yet are still at working age? And what about those who are on the streets? The street people concept is a relatively new phenomenon for the United States, which emerged during the past thirty years or so. These are only a few of the questions that need to be raised and carefully examined.

In order to understand these concepts more clearly, first the two extremes regarding the American enterprise system need to be articulated. Articulated by Gaski (1985) powerfully, he first states that the market is a natural equilibrium and as such it is sacrosanct. If left alone it will perform perfectly well. It is a product of almost a divine dispensation. Dugger (1989) points out that such beliefs lead to "enabling myths"; "sacrosanctity" and "perfectness" of the market are myths but they enable the upper strata in society to maintain dominance over the lower strata. He further maintains that those who benefit from the institutionalized status quo (a critical conservative position), believe that they benefit because their personal gifts or efforts merit it. So the status quo reflects a natural balance that is not to be interfered with. He further points out, however, that those who are for the status quo and the natural balance of the market are ignoring two simple facts: (1) people are educable, and (2) many people do not have equal opportunity (Samli 1992).

The other point of view is, again, stated by Dugger (1989). He points out that the market is an instituted process. This proposition takes the market's sacrosanctity away. If the market is an instituted process, then those who institute it can be held responsible. Further, the unchecked market does not remain the same. Those who have power gain more power and those who don't become somewhat desperate. The unchecked market does not provide opportunities to everyone, does not provide encouragement for those who are disadvantaged to begin with. This second position regarding our market system presents the essence of this book. The market needs certain strategic pushes and pulls in order to perform better for all. It simply cannot do everything all by itself. The market does not think and does not plan. It has no mind or consciousness.

THE PREVAILING DERAILMENT OF AMERICAN MARKETS

At this time, the American economy appears to be alright. However, deep down a sinister derailment of American markets is going on. This derailment is primarily based on the first point of view of the prevailing American markets—that is, they are not only natural, but are almost sacrosanct. By not interfering with them and by letting them work without outside interference, these markets will yield the best results. But as we leave the market alone, a series of structural changes are taking place and representing a derailment process in the American economy.

This derailment process is likely to create a major dilemma for the American consumer in the short run, and weaken the total industrial fabric of society in the long run. The next section explores factors causing the derailment.

These statements indicate how critical the situation is (these are just a few existing problems; more could be listed):

- Americans are paying far more for less choice.
- Americans are paying more for lesser quality service.
- Americans are allowing a runaway banking system that is using their money, paying almost no interest and charging them exorbitant fees.
- Americans are locked into a medical system in such a way that they are constantly paying more for less and less service.
- With the exception of top executives and certain other privileged few, Americans are not holding their own. Job security is low, other options for horizontal or upward vertical moves are limited. Indeed many are not able to make ends meet.
- As technological changes take place and jobs become more demanding, Americans cannot find time and do not have easy access to "skill improvement" opportunities.

Thus American consumers are not gaining any power. Instead, they are losing it steadily and systematically.

Exhibit I-1 illustrates the factors causing and the impact of the derailment of American markets on the consumer. As can be seen, the dilemma that American consumers are facing is caused by a number of underlying, far-reaching and long-lasting factors. Although many aspects of Exhibit I-1 must be discussed in detail, in this review chapter only a brief discussion of the exhibit will identify the underlying factors that are creating very difficult conditions for American consumers.

About the middle two-fifths of the American society is composed of mainstream Americans. This is the middle class. They are reasonably well educated with white-collar or specialized and highly skilled blue-collar jobs, making around $35–75,000 a year. This group is pressured by the financial community, paying exorbitant interest rates on their credit cards, paying excessive fees to banks who are already using this group's money almost for free. Exorbitant professional insurance premiums, and premiums on cars and homes are all making life very difficult.

Exhibit I-1
The Dilemma of the Mainstream American Consumer

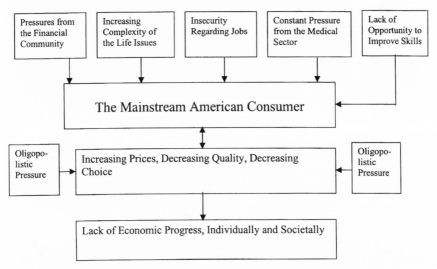

For this group a particularly important problem area is increasing complexity of life. The tax system; the communication system including TV, telephone and the Internet; the shopping system including shopping centers and telemarketing; the environmental protection or greening of consumption systems are all contributing to this complexity.

Large proportions of mainstream Americans are lower or middle managers. With the constant threats of downsizing, mergers and unfriendly takeovers, this sector is feeling very insecure. Mainstream Americans who are in this group feel as if they could lose their jobs any day. Such pressures are not conducive to creative hard work and increasing productivity. Instead of devoting themselves to their work, they are quite busy with identifying alternative employment opportunities for themselves. This is taking up tremendous time and energy. Similarly, because they are forced to change jobs often, they are not becoming a part of synergistic groups that are productive as a total unit rather than numerous unconnected individuals. These pressures are causing much loss to American industrial fabric as well as to individuals.

As Americans live longer their medical bills are also becoming larger. The complexity of medical payments, the high costs of copayments and profit-driven medical service deliverers are all creating a tremendous burden particularly on mainstream Americans who have aging parents and less-than-adequate medical insurance. The profit-driven medical insurance companies are taking one-third of all of medical expenditures without delivering any medical service. This situation is making this group almost helpless, since they have more difficulty taking care of aging parents as well as themselves. The medical service costs of this group are increasing faster than their incomes. Of course this is only part of the picture. At the time of writing this book an estimated 40 million Americans cannot even get medical insurance.

Closely related to their job situation, mainstream Americans are also facing constant change in their high-tech-related job complexities. Pressures to learn new skills are offset by pressures to work long and hard hours to keep their jobs. If they don't lose their jobs because of downsizing or takeovers, they are losing them by becoming out of touch in their high-tech jobs. Thus, the lack of opportunities to improve skills is creating a nightmarish situation. Mainstream Americans are losing power and status. The lowest fifth of our population, often referred to as the "working poor," who are more in the areas of unskilled blue-collar or minimum-wage-earning jobs never had any power to begin with and are experiencing worsening conditions.

BIG IS NOT BEAUTIFUL

The Impact of Oligopolies

Most of the factors discussed above that are creating the consumer dilemma are caused by a major development, concentration of economic power. During the past two decades there has been a considerable concentration of economic power leading to emergence of powerful oligopolies. The emergence of these oligopolies is causing a major reduction in competition, which, in turn, is leading to increasing prices, decreasing quality and decreasing choice. In fact it is possible to claim that all of the factors causing the dilemma of mainstream consumers discussed in Exhibit I-1 can be causally related to the oligopolistic tendencies of the American industry.

The outcome of oligopolistic tendencies leads to a lack in economic progress since:

- Incomes of large masses are neglected in favor of a few high-level executives.
- Competition is reduced and/or, in some cases, eliminated.
- Research and development activities are reduced so that the company resources can be used for buying out the competition.

- Human resource development efforts in companies have been reduced.
- Economic power has spilled into political power in such a way that most progressive ideas are blocked in favor of maintaining the *status quo*.

Thus, big is not beautiful and perhaps must be stopped from getting too much bigger and becoming a burden on the American society. American markets, because of the tendency on the part of the big getting bigger, are being moved steadily from "survival of the fittest" to "survival of the fattest." Much of this tendency and the resultant enlargement of major American firms can be traced to the prevailing merger mania.

Merger Mania and American Markets

As Marino (1997) states:

I predict that today's merger mania will be tomorrow's spinoff schizophrenia. It's astounding and confusing as the chief executive who asked his operating management to write a business plan for plumbing and examine the potential profits in Mississippi, without telling them whether he meant the state or the river.

Merger mania has been going on throughout the 1990s and is accelerating. There was a time (approximately in the 1950s and early 1960s) when companies bought out other companies that were at the brink of bankruptcy and they operated these companies. In today's merger mania, very large companies that are not efficient and not very profitable are buying off their leanest and meanest competitors to look good and to eliminate competition. Marino (1997) calls merger mania an exercise in self-gratification. However, I take a different point of view. I believe it is an attempt to destroy the industrial fabric of the American society. These people ask the government to eliminate the regulatory burdens (Gatty 1995) and then go ahead and buy out their competition. Hence, reduce or eliminate competition and become more ineffective and inefficient because of their obscene fatness. The old adage of "if you cannot lick them you join them" is revised as "if you cannot lick them you buy them."

The companies that are heavily engaged in merger mania are becoming oligopolistic and causing major problems for consumers. In addition to the regular problems caused by oligopolistic conditions—that is, being removed from consumers, being too large and inflexible—these companies are losing track of their core competencies and are becoming ineffective in the marketplace. Furthermore, they may discontinue some of their key products as they shift their focus to other products (Goldberg 1997). This would further cause problems for consumers by limiting their choice.

Is Piracy Legal?

Piracy is illegal anywhere else in the world, but is legal on Wall Street. Leveraged buyouts and unfriendly takeovers attest to that. Unfortunately, the fat can freely buy out the lean and nothing can be done about it. Empowerment of American consumers is dependent on how much power the fat are allowed to have. By allowing the piracy to continue on Wall Street, the power of the consumer is minimized. This is the derailment of American markets.

SUMMARY

American markets are being derailed and American consumers are facing a constantly escalating dilemma. These problems are not quite so obvious to the naked eye when the economy is doing well. However, if and when there is a recession or a down cycle in the economy, the results will be devastating. American consumers, among others, are being pressured by the financial community, the increasing complexity of the society, job insecurities, the medical sector and finally, the lack of opportunities to improve skills. Behind most of these problems is the unbelievable concentration of economic power in the hands of a few firms. These firms are creating oligopolistic pressures that are leading in the direction of increasing prices, decreasing quality and decreasing choice. These conditions do not allow American markets to capitalize on their full potential. Hence, the economy does not grow satisfactorily. American consumers need not lose more power; on the contrary, they need to be empowered in order for the economy to make progress.

REFERENCES

Blanchard, Ken; Carlos, John P.; and Randolph, Alan (1996). *Empowerment Takes More Than a Minute*. San Francisco: Berrett-Koehler Publishers.

Davis, Keith (1975). "Five Propositions for Social Responsibility," *Business Horizons*, June, 19–24.

Dugger, William M. (1989). "Instituted Process and Enabling Myth: The Two Faces of the Market," *Journal of Economic Issues*, June, 607–615.

Gaski, John F. (1985). "Dangerous Territory: The Social Marketing Concept Revisited," *Business Horizons*, July/August, 42–47.

Gatty, Bob (1995). "Congress Seeks to Relieve Regulatory Burdens," *Beverage Industry*, February, 21–22.

Goldberg, Aaron (1997). "Beware Effects of Merger Mania," *PC Week*, July, 69–70.

Marino, Sal (1997). "From Merger Mania to Spinoff Schizophrenia," *Industry Week*, January 20, 30–31.

Moore, James F. (1996). *The Death of Competition*. New York: HarperCollins.

Samli, A. Coskun (1992). *Social Responsibility in Marketing*. Westport, CT: Quorum Books.

Thurow, Lester (1996). *The Future of Capitalism*. New York: Penguin Books.

_____ **Chapter 1**

Accumulation of Economic Power

INTRODUCTION

The key tenet of capitalism is competition. Competition keeps the economy going. It stimulates investments, productivity, research and development. It creates economic growth and wealth, and, above all, it creates consumer satisfaction. Consumer satisfaction here is related to choice, quality and availability of goods and services. All of these are products of healthy competition. After all, if businesses are fighting for consumer dollars, they will have to make consumers happy. However, if the economic power in a society is concentrated in the hands of a few businesses or a few families, there is no room for competition. These powerful businesses, instead of going out of their way to satisfy consumer needs, simply dictate to the consumers what to buy. A "buy or don't buy, that is all we've got" attitude prevails. In this day and age of a new economic world order, if a company, industry or country does not compete in global markets, it is almost doomed. If competition is deteriorating within a country, this makes that country less competitive in global markets also. This chapter presents a discussion of the concentration of economic power in the American economy and the resultant reduction in domestic competition. It is further discussed that the reduction of competition in the home front significantly reduces the country's global competitiveness.

CREATING WEALTH

Despite what some philosophers would claim, that in the end economics is not about material progress but pursuit of happiness (Krugman 1998), 30 million Americans who do not know where and when the next meal is coming from, or every sixth child who lives in poverty would not quite agree. The economy must create wealth. In the words of Drucker (1999, p. 116), "enterprises are paid to create wealth, not to control cost" is the economic reality of our system. But Drucker's position is not quite sufficient; wealth should not accumulate in the hands of a few privileged organizations or individuals, it must reach out and touch all bar none in the society. This is not advocating economic equality but equality in economic opportunity. Giving individuals the tools to improve themselves and live up to the maximum of their potential, thus giving them equality in economic opportunity, is basically equated in this book to empowering the consumer and creating a kinder and gentler atmosphere for all to improve themselves.

Just how do we create economic well-being and wealth? Exhibit 1–1 illustrates a model originally developed by Thurow (1999) and modified by this author. There are six points to the model. Although many of these points are discussed throughout this book, a brief description of this author's perspective is in order.

The first and perhaps the most basic step in the model is related to creating and maintaining public order, which will give rise to better education, better infrastructures and better health care services. Without these basics society cannot even begin to make progress.

But if the first step is fulfilled, then we need people with initiatives who are entrepreneurs. They think there are other ways of doing business that can compete by improving products, services and processes.

Simultaneously, society must create opportunity for innovations, breakthroughs and particularly application of scientific and technological advancements to the economy. Opportunity to advance science and technology must be created, it cannot be happening all by itself. It has been stated, for instance, that 73 percent of the private patents in our society were based on knowledge generated by public sources such as universities and government laboratories. Although we cannot possibly afford it, because of political pressures the U.S. government is cutting down this vital support for research and development (Thurow 1999).

Exhibit 1–1
Creating Wealth in a Society

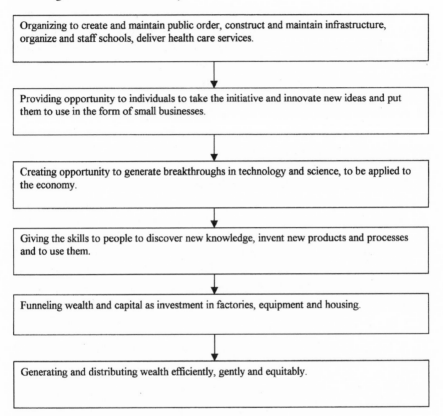

Organizing to create and maintain public order, construct and maintain infrastructure, organize and staff schools, deliver health care services.
Providing opportunity to individuals to take the initiative and innovate new ideas and put them to use in the form of small businesses.
Creating opportunity to generate breakthroughs in technology and science, to be applied to the economy.
Giving the skills to people to discover new knowledge, invent new products and processes and to use them.
Funneling wealth and capital as investment in factories, equipment and housing.
Generating and distributing wealth efficiently, gently and equitably.

Source: Adapted and revised from Thurow (1999).

Once technological knowledge is generated, people must be given the skills to apply this knowledge. There must be invention of new products and new processes and people must be able to use them.

At this stage, society must pour wealth and capital as investment into critical areas. Factories, equipment, housing and other necessary factors of production must be in place for economic growth and they should receive much of these investments.

All of these steps must be in the direction of environmentally friendly efforts. Unlike some extreme thinking, without a safe environment and eco-logical balance, the economy cannot survive in the long run. When the whole society's well-being is at stake we cannot worry about the short run only.

Finally, and most important, the fruits and benefits of all of these economic activities must be shared. The wealth that is generated must be distributed not among the wealthy or privileged few, but among the whole society. Not equally, but equitably, for this, among others, we must maintain our competitiveness at home and learn to treat consumers kindly and gently. Perhaps one thing we cannot and should not do is to hope and pray that there is in former President Reagan's way of thinking enough "trickle down" from rich to the poor. Trickle down is not a good proposition because it implies that the rich are taking care of the underclass at their own discretion. Income inequality at the time of writing this book is plaguing the U.S. economy. The most recent data (Koretz 2000) indicate that there is no trickle down. On the contrary, the income of the top 5 percent of our families jumped 18.3 times ahead of the bottom 20 percent. These growth figures for the top 5 percent are accelerating. In the 1970s this discrepancy in relative increases was only 11 times as opposed to 18.3 times in the 1990s (Koretz 2000).

For all of these wealth-related facts to come together as shown in Exhibit 1–1, all parties involved—the government, the private sector and the population—must cooperate. Competition must be maintained at home and in the global markets.

GLOBAL COMPETITIVENESS BEGINS AT HOME

International competitiveness of nations, according to some, is an illusive concept (Waheeduzzaman and Ryans 1996), but also a major national concern. It is the degree to which a nation can, under free and fair market conditions, produce better goods and services for international markets while real incomes of the citizenry are maintained or expanded. Thus, the competitiveness of a nation is not an end but a means to an end. The ultimate goal of international competitiveness is to maintain and increase real incomes of the people and, hence, to increase the standard of living for them. Thus it means the ability to create, produce, distribute and/or service products in international trade (Scott and Lodge 1985). Most similar definitions fail to include two extremely critical ingredients that are particularly important in today's international competitiveness: effective marketing and managerial superiority.

Effective Marketing

As Thurow (1992, p. 30) stated: "What was an era of niche competition in the last half of the twentieth century will become an era of head-to-head competition in the first half of the twenty-first century." In niche competition, country A bought widgets from country B because they were the best for the price. And in return country B bought from country A another product that it could not produce efficiently. Thus both parties were better off. However, in head-to-head competition all products and services are on the table. Both countries are competing for almost everything and not necessarily on an economic basis.

Therefore, while niche competition is win-win, head-to-head competition is win-lose. Thus, effective marketing becomes extremely critical (Samli 1995). Understanding the unique differences of international market segments and catering to these specific needs is much more complicated than simple international trade practices. This change in orientation is a *must* for survival in the win-lose situation described by Thurow.

Managerial Superiority

In order to understand managerial superiority, it is necessary to examine the classical trade theories of *comparative advantage* and *competitive advantage*.

The theory of comparative advantage, which is credited to Ricardo (1817), advocates that a country will produce and export those goods and services with which it has comparative advantage in price or factor cost (as both are key elements of trade). In fact, the reason for trading, according to comparative advantage theory, is the comparative advantage that a country has in relative price and factor inputs. In classical economic theory, this kind of trade based on comparative advantage is very beneficial to all parties involved. In all cases, it creates more jobs, stimulates the economy, helps expand the economic base and creates an international division of labor, encouraging concentration in the areas in where each country has comparative advantage.

Competitive advantage is a more recent concept, which has two diametrically opposing positions. According to some, competitive advantage (Waheeduzzaman and Ryans 1996; Durand and Giorno 1987; Anderton and Dunnett 1987) is a subset of comparative advantage. According to these thinkers, the competitiveness of a nation depends on its advantages in the relative price of goods and services in the international marketplace. This is a strictly classical way of thinking. Much effort has been made to determine countries' competitiveness by measuring their export prices or production costs or by summarizing their export-import competitiveness (Waheeduzzaman and Ryans 1996).

The other approach to competitive advantage may be credited to Porter (1990) or Thurow (1992) among others. If international trade is going in the direction of win-lose, then it is necessary to explore other aspects of competitiveness.

Classical economics was focused on labor, capital and resources in terms of their comparative characteristics. It was posited that as a result of the advantages in these factors of production, trade takes place. It was Porter (1990) who articulated strategic aspects of management and subsequently managerial superiority. Porter identified generic strategies. He maintained that the firm's competitiveness can be enhanced by creating focus on specific markets, by differentiating the firm from its competitors and by creating a cost or price leadership. All of these are based on management skills and not the size of the company. Both Porter and Thurow indicate that *managerial superiority* as a critical factor of production is going to play a more critical role in trade. This is completely out of the conceptual frame of classicists, neoclassical thinkers and other like-minded people.

The first approach to competitive advantage encourages financial or resource superiority that may be obtained by expanding a company's size. This is partly the reason for the merger mania that is going on in American markets. This indeed may provide competitive advantage in the *short run* by emphasizing superiority through newly acquired financial and physical resources.

The second approach to competitive advantage maintains that it is not an extension of comparative advantage. In fact, totally to the contrary, competitive advantage has its own base in managerial competency. Consider, for instance, a small city-state such as Singapore. It does not have vast resources or large sums of capital; however, thanks to its hard-working, educated people and competent managers, it pulled itself from "rags" to "riches" during the 1970s, 1980s and 1990s. In fact, in 1997 Singapore was rated first in the world for excelling in almost every major area that counts in terms of competitiveness (*Franchising World* 1997). America is still reasonably competitive, but its competitiveness is eroding as it allows merger mania to continue. That is, if we accept that the second approach to competitive advantage is more realistic and knowing that merger mania deals only with size and resources but not managerial superiority, then we realize that it is helping erode national competitiveness (Samli and Jacobs 1995).

Porter (1990) maintained that unless the country keeps its competitiveness at its home front, it cannot compete globally with other nations. Thus, maintaining and enhancing competitiveness is very critical. Large American companies have been and are extremely busy buying each other out. While part of the theory of comparative advantage states that this will provide competitiveness, this is likely to be short-lived unless managerial superiority is constantly cultivated. Some small companies and some small states and, of course, small countries are trying to achieve competitiveness through competitive advantage by cultivating further their human resource development and trying to achieve managerial superiority. More on competitive versus comparative advantage is presented in chapter 9.

MERGER MANIA LEADS TO OLIGOPOLIES

Just what happens, for instance, when two giant banks merge? Let us explore the case of NationsBank that bought out Barnett Bank. First of all, these two banks treat their customers very differently. In many parts of Florida, they were located in close proximity, but consumers chose one or the other, but not simply one. Banking is a people business. People need choices as to where to bank and even how to bank. Consumers need people in the bank to talk to and to conduct business. Nevertheless, NationsBank announced that in order to reduce expenses to help pay for the deal it would cut more than 6,000 jobs. Assume, for instance, that each one of these people who were about to be laid off catered to 100 people per day. Some 600,000 people would not receive the attention they were used to receiving daily. There cannot be any benefit to the consumer in this sense. When the spokesperson for the bank stated that the merger with Barnett "added momentum and focus on serving the needs of our customers," she could not have been serious. Additionally, NationsBank is closing dozens, if not hundreds, of commercial credit centers and branches across the country, further removing itself from its markets (Bennett 1998). Furthermore, this merger is reducing consumers' choice of banks drastically.

Recent experience has shown that after just about every bank merger, there has been a reduction in services and increase in fees (Perman 1998). This is simply one example of merger mania that has been plaguing the American economy. It will be very difficult to believe that the merger between NationsBank and Barnett Bank is of any benefit to their own customers, to the market and to consumers in general. With the exception of a few administrators at the top, and perhaps some shareholders, there are no clearcut beneficiaries of this merger activity.

Typical of almost all mergers, it is not the stakeholders (consumers and society as a whole) but only some of the stockholders who are likely to benefit from this merger activity. Additionally, small companies argue that their very large rivals are using extremely aggressive strategies to kill the competition coming from their small rivals. Five such practices are typically cited (*Business Week* 1998).

Tying. Manufacturers demand the purchase of their other products (e.g., Microsoft has been accused of tying its operating system to its Internet browser).

Market-Share Discounts. The purchaser gets big discounts as it gives more and more of its business to the manufacturer.

Slotting fees. Particularly common in the food-and-beverage industry, these fees are used to gain exclusive shelf space at supermarkets.

Bundled Rebates. When a buyer purchases more than one product it gets rebates. Some of the goods in the rebate bundle may be in very high demand. This is similar to tying.

Exclusivity incentives. Any form of payments such as advertising for a promise not to buy from the competitors.

As indicated in this merger episode, companies eliminate competition through mergers and they become more oligopolistic, and subsequently even monopolistic. The scope of merger mania in the United States is mind-boggling. During 1996 there were 2,670 mergers amounting to $556,308 million (or $556 billion). Exhibit 1–2 indicates some of these more important mergers. As can be seen, the activity spread into many major industries.

In terms of the dollar value of mergers, the telecommunications industry was number one in 1996. The electric gas and water distribution industry was second, with a value of over $40 billion. By looking at the 1996 figures, one may think that these are very large numbers. However, the 1997 merger mania showed a tremendous increase over 1996 dollars: total merger mania dollars in 1997 reached $653.5 billion. The 1998 merger mania figures were not completely available. At the same time, the merger mania in 1998 showed some of the largest transactions, as shown in Exhibit 1–2. Emphasizing a simple semiaverage method, using half of the number of observation years for projecting into the future, a trend analysis was performed. In our case by using merger data for 1985 through 1997, twelve years, we projected six years into the future. According to our estimates, by the year 2003, the total value of all mergers will be over $2 trillion. This number may be approaching or exceeding the total budget of the U.S. government, and there seems to be no relief in sight.

However, all industries are not becoming oligopolistic at the same rate. Some industries are controlled by three or four companies up to 100 percent. Exhibit 1–3 gives a list of the ten most oligopolistic industries and the level of concentration of the largest firms in these industries. It is not clear how oligopolistic the industries listed in Exhibit 1–3 are or will be. However, this

Exhibit 1–2
Mergers and Acquisitions in the United States

A - Industry mergers ranked by volume and quantity for 1996

Industry	Rank	$ Amount (mil $)	Nb of Businesses	Rank
Telecommunications	1	77,814.6	58	14
Electric, gas, water distribution	2	40,355.2	41	17
Radio & Television broadcasting stations	3	32,064.5	178	3
Business Services	4	28,632.8	263	1
Transportation & Shipping (except Air)	5	28,266.4	51	15
Oil & Gas: Petroleum Refining	6	26,018.1	138	4
Commercial banks, bank holding companies	7	21,259.2	185	2
Measuring, Medical, Photo equipment; clocks	8	21,064.8	92	7
Aerospace and Aircraft	9	19,628.1	10	36
Hotels and Casinos	10	13,991.1	135	5

Source: U.S. Census Bureau. Table 885 *Mergers and Acquisitions, by industry:* 1996
Securities Data Company, Newark, NJ, Merger & Corporate Transactions Database.

B - Industry Mergers 1997

- Monster Year for M & A: **772 transactions in the U.S. for a Value of $653.5 billion**.
- (a third more deals and 40% more dollars than 1996)
- The biggest deal of 1997 was WorldCom's $35.3 billion acquisition of MCI Communications.
- Banking, Brokerage, Investment banking and Insurance transactions accounted for nearly one-third of all deals in 1997.

C - Mergers & Acquisitions for 1998

Largest announced U.S. Mergers, Acquisitions and Spinoffs in 1998

- Citicorp bought by Travelers Group Inc.: Value of the transaction: $72,558.2 million
- Ameritech Corp bought by SBC Communications: Value of the transaction: $72,356.5 million
- GTE Corp bought by Bell Atlantic Corp.: Value of the transaction: $70,873.6 million

whole trend appears to be a major decline in the competitiveness of American industries. Just what happens to these oligopolistic industries?

Oligopolies Are Dinosaurs

Perhaps most important, these very large firms are not competing in the traditional manner. They are not interested in being engaged in a price competition that should help the ultimate consumer. Oligopolists avoid price competition, which will eventually become a price war. Because of the very nature of oligopolies, these firms will lose much in such price wars. This takes away their ability to compete and provide the benefits of price competition to consumers.

There are additional problems (or indeed ailments) that oligopolists develop, and they cannot get out of these problem situations. These problem

Exhibit 1–3
Concentration Levels in Various Product Markets

Product Category	Largest Firms	Concentration Ratio (%)
Instant Breakfast	Carnation, Pillsbury, Dean Foods	100
Tennis Balls	Penn, Wilson, Dunlap, Spalding	100
Disposable Diapers	Procter & Gamble, Kimberly-Clark, Curity, Romar	99
Breakfast Cereals	Kellogg, General Mills, Philip Morris, Quaker Oats	98
Cameras and Film	Eastman Kodak, Polaroid, Bell & Howell, Berkey	98
Chewing Gum	Wrigley, Warner-Lambert, Squibb, Philip Morris	97
Electric Razors	Norelco, Remington, Warner-Lambert, Sunbeam	96
Sanitary Napkins	Johnson & Johnson, Kimberly-Clark, Procter & Gamble	96
Batteries	Duracell, Eveready, Ray-O-Vac, Kodak	94
Soft Drinks	Coca-Cola, Pepsi-Cola, Cadbury Schweppes, Royal Crown	93

Source: Adapted and revised from Schiller (1997).

areas can be identified as flexibility, market sensitivity, R&D performance, core-competency and overall effectiveness.

Flexibility. American oligopolies are so large that it is difficult to even imagine how they could react to unexpected developments in the market-place or how they could take advantage of newly emerging opportunities. In other words, as they become larger, the firms become less flexible.

Some years ago, George Romney, president of American Motors and sub-sequently the governor of Michigan, stated that General Motors (GM) is so big that it cannot function efficiently. It must be broken into five separate companies which must compete with each other. How little did Mr. Romney know that, some thirty years later, GM had to lay off about 70,000 workers, which, I believe, was one of a kind in terms of magnitude. At the time, I reiterated the fact that, in history, even emperors did not have such raw power to dismiss so many workers or put to death so many people. I always imagined what would happen if these 70,000 workers were to march to the GM headquarters in Detroit and tell the management: "No, You Are Fired."

It is constantly amazing to me that these oligopolists talk about how the U.S. government is so large that it is ineffective and inefficient, while they are almost as big or bigger. It is quite reasonable to posit that corporate entities have maximum size limitations. Early in the twentieth century, numerous attempts were made by economists to establish the specifics of these size limitations, and partially because of these attempts antitrust legislation was put in place. One point is amply clear: the larger the organization, the more bureaucracy it needs and the less flexibility it has to move fast, to respond quickly and to accomplish anything swiftly.

Market Sensitivity. If consumers do not have many viable options, they cannot switch. Buying out the competition, by definition, eliminates consumer options and hence diminishes the possibilities for consumers to switch to other brands or change businesses or services. If consumers do not have many options, the business does not feel the necessity to be sensitive to consumer needs, since customers have no place to go. These large giants who have captured portions of the market do not have any need to improve, to be more responsive to consumer needs or enhance their sensitivity to predict the forthcoming needs of the consuming public. One very critical and related area needs to be further discussed here. As mergers take place, many well-paying middle-management jobs are eliminated. And many others are reduced both in numbers and in pay. It is quite likely that good-quality high-paying jobs are not generated quickly and adequately. In fact, a study reports that most of the jobs created in the first decade of the twenty-first century will be relatively low paying low jobs. Exhibit 1–4 indicates that much of the job creation will be in the areas of cashiers, retail sales persons, teacher aides and the like. Certainly, this type of trend will not have a positive impact in the economic well-being of American consumers.

R&D Performance. When a giant company has captured a large chunk of the market and has a good cash position, it feels no obligation to explore the unknown and commit large resources on research and development (R&D). In other words, large size may interfere with society's opportunities to reach out and develop better products and services. If this happens, everybody loses.

Unfortunately, companies that are extensively involved in mergers and acquisitions put most of their resources into these merger-related areas. They stay away from "iffy" basic research or costly R&D projects. Most giant corporations have top managements who need to have high profiles

Exhibit 1–4
America's Expected Job Growth in Some of the Key Areas for the Decade of 1996–2006

Cashiers	530,000	•Low income category
Systems Analysts	520,000	
General Managers and top Executives	467,000	
Registered Nurses	411,000	
Retail Sales Persons	408,000	•Low income category
Truck Drivers	404,000	
Home Health Aids	378,000	
Teacher Aids	370,000	•Low income category

Source: Adapted and revised from *Business Week* January 26, 1998, 22.

and need to show profits in the short run. Since R&D is mainly a long-term proposition, and since basic research is a very high-cost gambling activity, the managements of these giants are not very interested in the R&D-related activities.

Core Competency. Small or large firms all have certain core competency areas in which they excel. In fact, these competency areas are their bread and butter, and help maintain their existence. Much of the time, mergers, acquisitions and unfriendly takeovers lead in the direction of diversification. Certainly, under particular circumstances, diversification can be quite beneficial. However, many American giants that are engaged in mergers leading to diversification have discovered that they have gotten away from their core competency areas. As a result, many of these companies have lost much money. Perhaps the best example here is Sears. After having been the number-one merchandiser for over half a century, Sears got engaged in big-time diversification. It got into banking, real estate insurance and other major financial activities to a point where it lost its focus and got away from its core competency areas. The end result was major financial losses for the company. It had to regroup and go back to its core competency area, which is merchandising. Many companies did not even have a chance to go back to their core competency. They just became derailed from their markets, were ineffective and some of them even died.

Overall Effectiveness. It is very difficult to claim an increased effectiveness as companies continue their merger and acquisition activities. According to one theory, if two companies have the same core competencies and they merge, then one and one may not be equal to two, but only to one and a

Exhibit 1-5
The Key Features of Sameness

Feature	Organizational Implications	Consumer Implications
Inflexible	Focused on itself and has difficulties to change	Cannot take care of most changing needs
Unlearning	Not enough continuity in learning from experiences since there is high degree of managerial turnover	Has difficulty understanding how and why consumers behave
Isolated	Internally oriented	Does not even know what the consumers want
Unfocused	Much emphasis on understanding competitors and counteracting	Not at all consumer oriented, and knows very little of consumer needs and desires

half. This is because they try to cut costs, downsize and eliminate some of the duplication. None of these particularly help consumers. However, as the theory posits, if the two companies have complementary skills and know-how, and they decide to merge, then there is a possibility of generating *synergy*. Since many mergers are sameness plus sameness, they are not making a net contribution to the well-being of society ("Sizing Up the Merger Mania" 1997).

When mergers take place based on "sameness," at least four characteristics become prevalent: inflexibility, unlearning, isolation and lack of focus (Exhibit 1-5). Those large companies that are merging on the sameness basis become inflexible. Inflexibility relates to the size and complexity of the bureaucracy that the company has to maintain to run itself. These companies cannot react to quick changes in the marketplace. They cannot make quick decisions and properly inform different components of their organization. Thus a lack of congruity sets in, and the organization becomes dysfunctional.

The large companies that merge on the sameness basis lay off people, eliminate some organizational layers and create discontinuity in their organizational communications. Therefore, what is learned by some managers doesn't travel throughout the organization. Thus, organizational learning does not take place.

Isolatedness here refers to being far removed from consumers and not being close to the markets in general. The firm loses its alertness and ability to respond to market changes early. The end result is a loss in profitability and competitiveness. Furthermore, isolatedness also causes inability to take advantage of new opportunities that may emerge in the markets due to sudden and significant changes in the markets (Samli 1993).

Finally, as fewer and fewer competitors remain in the marketplace as a result of mergers, competitors become more visible. Firms begin emphasizing or imitating their competitors' behaviors and their competitive activities. This is not necessarily bad in itself; however, as this pattern emerges, it takes away a firm's focus on competing in the marketplace and creating better quality and service for customers. Rather, the focus moves into competing head on with a few key competitors and trying to outsmart them. This behavior certainly does not generate the consumer value that typically accrues through competition.

Too Much Economic Power

Economic power of a firm is related to its size, its productive capability and its share of the total market. But it is also a determinant of how much the firm may invest to renovate or expand, how much the firm may spend in acquiring other businesses, how much the firm will invest in R&D, how many employees it will have and many other economic power-related decisions that play a critical role in the regional, national or international economies as well as in the lives of many people.

Economic Power Begets Economic Power

Economic power begets power, but not necessarily efficiency or consumer benefit. Economic power can be a reflection of competitive power but not necessarily consumer benefit. Booth and Philip (1998) discuss the emergence of two different schools of thought on competitiveness: technology-driven and competency-driven approaches. The technology-driven approach stresses the importance of information technology, and the competency-driven approach deals with managerial superiority. The authors maintain that the technology-driven approach is an important source of advantage against competitors. This advantage is strictly a function of size. Larger companies have much easier access to information technology, which further enhances their advantageous position. The more size-oriented the firms become, the more they emphasize the technology-driven approach.

The competency-driven approach emphasizes vigorous planning and the use of generic strategies. It goes in the direction of managerial superiority. With widespread mergers and resultant downsizing, high rates of managerial turnover have been playing havoc among the managerial ranks. As managers move to other positions or are laid off, the firm loses its core competencies.

Management teams do not remain together long enough to develop higher levels of competency. As a result, there is less and less successful implementation of the competency-driven approach to competitiveness.

Buying Out the Mean and the Lean

Perhaps one of the worst impacts of the current merger mania is seen in different industries in the form of changing overall effectiveness. In the past, mergers and acquisitions meant buying out those companies that were not doing well and were perhaps at the brink of bankruptcy. Making these companies functional and profitable meant a significant contribution to the well-being of the American economy. Through mergers and acquisitions, dysfunctional firms used to become very functional and contribute to the economy through their enhanced ability to compete, generate better products and services and create jobs.

However, the corporate raiders of the 1980s and 1990s have been using a totally different orientation. They target the leanest and meanest small competitors and buy them out. Much of the time these newly acquired businesses are partially dismantled. They are no longer as effective as they were before the acquisition. The outcome of such mergers and acquisitions is basically weakening the industrial fabric of society. Instead of lean, mean machines trying to compete further and improve their performance, now they are purchased by a giant that wants them, basically, out of the way, not competing and creating a headache. Thus smaller and efficient competitors do not actually have a chance to achieve optional maturity and perform according to their maximum capability. A continuous pattern of this type cannot help but chip away at society's industrial power and its potential progress.

Free Markets and Not So Free Entry

Perhaps one of the most critical problems generated by the "oligopolization" of American economy is the freedom of entry. If an industry is controlled by a few very large firms, not only a "business is as usual" atmosphere sets in, but it cannot even be changed by outside challenge. It is almost impossible to enter the market by an outsider. The American automotive industry has been in this position for a long time. The only outside competition has come through imports, which is not quite the same thing. Only one major attempt in the United States was Delorian cars in the late 1970s. The attempt failed primarily because of the lack of resources to compete with the existing oligopolists. For years it was expected that General Electric would enter the market with an electric car, but again for the same reason, this has not happened.

In oligopolistic industries (with the current trends, in almost all major industries), entering the market would mean the availability of resources to compete with giants who are quite well established. In such cases entering the market is almost like suicide and, if the firm can enter, it is easier for it to *conform* to the practices of other oligopolists than to rock the boat and challenge them.

Thus the commonly used phrase, *the free market*, becomes very questionable. The less free the market, the greater potential exists for exploitation of consumers. The benefits of capitalism, therefore, dissipate. Garten (1999) describes the situation as the era of big government being superseded by the age of global goliaths. These big companies have disproportionate clout on national legislation in such a way that there is a growing imbalance between private and public power in our society. The superlarge corporations that are the result of the on-going merger mania are not likely to focus as intensely as smaller companies do on support for local neighborhoods, schools, the arts, the development of research activities and, above all, the well-being of consumers.

SUMMARY

This chapter points out a few conditions that would enhance consumer well-being, but the trends are strictly in the direction of elimination of these conditions. First, it is posited that American competitiveness is dissipating, which is detrimental to American global competitiveness. American firms are putting emphasis more on size and financial power (comparative advantage) rather than managerial superiority and, hence, competitive advantage. Furthermore, the decreasing competition in American economy is creating problems for the American consumer. Declining competition is primarily due to merger mania. The on-going and accelerating merger mania is leading toward creation of oligopolies. Oligopolists are inflexible, unlearning, isolated and unfocused. As a result, they are hardly looking after the consumers' best interest. Additionally, as industries become more oligopolistic, a barrier is set against new entrants in the marketplace. Thus, American competition and competitiveness are on the decline, and American consumers are paying the price. Many of the points discussed in this chapter will be elaborated upon in subsequent chapters.

REFERENCES

Anderton, R. and Dunnett, A. (1987). "Modeling the Behavior of Export Volumes of Manufacturers: An Evaluation of the Performance of Different Measures of International Competitiveness," *National Institute Economic Review*, August, 46–52.

Bennett, Jane (1998). "NationsBank to Close 11 Credit Centers," *Jacksonville Business Journal*, 13, February, 49.

Booth, Marilyn E. and George Philip (1988). "Technology, Competencies and Competitiveness: The Case for Reconfigurble and Flexible Strategies," *Journal of Business Research*, January, 29–41.

Business Week (1998). "Are Corporate Predators on the Loose?" February 23, 124–128.

Drucker, Peter (1999). "Beyond the Information Revolution," *The Atlantic Monthly*, October.

Durand, Martine and Giorno, Claude, (1987). "Indicators of International Competitiveness: Conceptual Aspects and Evaluation," *OECD Economic Studies 9*, Autumn, 147–182.

Franchising World (1997). "Global Competitiveness Report," July–August, 47.

Garten, Jeffrey E. (1999). "Mega Mergers are a Clear and Present Danger," *Business Week*, January 25, 28.

Koretz, Gene (2000). "Economic Trends," *Business Week*, January 31, 34.

Krugman, Paul (1998). "Viagra and Wealth of Nations," *New York Times Magazine*, September 23, 24.

Perman, Stacy (1998). "Goodbye, Freebies—Hello Fees," *Time Magazine*, January 12, 40.

Porter, Michael (1990). *The Competitive Advantage of Nations*. New York: The Free Press.

Ricardo, David (1817). *On the Principles of Political Economy and Taxation*. London.

Samli, A. Coskun (1993). *Counterturbulence Marketing*. Westport, CT: Quorum Books.

Samli, A. Coskun (1995). *International Consumer Behavior*. Westport, CT: Quorum Books.

Samli, Coskun and Jacobs, Laurence (1995). "Achieving Congruence Between Macro and Micro Generic Strategies: A Framework to Create International Competitive Advantage," *Journal of Macromarketing*, Fall, 23–32.

Schiller, Bradley R. (1997). *The Micro Economy Today*. New York: McGraw-Hill.

Scott, Bruce R. and Lodge, George (1985). *U.S. Competitiveness in the World Economy*. Boston: Harvard Business School Press.

"Sizing Up the Merger Mania" (1997). *Management Review*, December, 37–42.

Thurow, Lester (1992). *Head to Head*. New York: William Morrow.

Thurow, Lester (1999). *Building Wealth*. New York: HarperCollins.

Waheeduzzaman, A. N. M. and Ryans, John K. Jr. (1996). "Definition Perspectives and Understanding of International Competitiveness: A Quest for a Common Ground," *Competitiveness Review*, 6 November, 7–26.

_____ **Chapter 2**

The Plight of the American Consumer

The strength of America has been the large size of its middle class that has provided, all along, stability to the economy. American markets have been large, and the presence of this middle class has been the key factor in creating large aggregate demand for most products. The size of this demand facilitated the emergence and continuation of mass production. This coexistence of mass production and mass consumption created a reasonably high level of quality of life to the masses.

However, unlike the past, American society is being divided into two Americas, rich and poor. Certainly, in terms of size, these two are not equal. While the poor America is becoming very large, the rich America has been very small (about 5 percent of the total American society).

The middle class, which in the past appeared to include almost all Americans, is simply not growing either in terms of numbers or purchasing power (Leonhardt 1997). Rather, it is the top and bottom ends of the American market that are swelling. Since 1980, the income of the wealthiest fifth of the American population grew by about 38 percent, while wages for the bottom 60 percent either stagnated or dropped further. Thus, there is a great polarization of income in the United States. If the upper 1 percent of the population is to be considered, these differences become significantly more pronounced. This group's net income growth is around or more than 130 percent (Samli 1993). Thus, there is a very noticeable erosion in traditional American mass markets, and the erosion is continuing (Leonhardt 1997). For example, if we define middle-class households as those with incomes ranging around the national average, we find that the share with incomes between $25,000 and $50,000 in 1994 dollars shrank from 38 percent in 1970 to 30 percent in 1994 (Kacapyr, Francese and Crispell 1996). It is quite likely that this trend is continuing.

One measure of how income is distributed in the United States is the Gini coefficient, an innovation of an Italian demographer, Corrodo Gini. It examines the overall distribution of income in a society. A Gini coefficient of 0 represents a perfectly equal distribution of income. It literally means everyone is in the middle class. A Gini coefficient of 1 indicates that all of the income goes to a single individual, household or family. That further means that no one else has any income. In modern industrial societies, the Gini coefficient has never approached these two extremes. However, the more it increases, the more it illustrates a deterioration in income distribution. The U.S. Gini coefficient has risen from .394 in 1970 to .456 in 1994 (Kacapyr, Francese and Crispell 1996).

This situation is primarily attributed to the stagnation in U.S. wages. Between 1971 and 1994, the average growth in U.S. real wages was only .3 percent per year. This is a significant decline from 2.5 percent that was experienced between 1955 and 1970 (Kacapyr, Francese and Crispell 1996). Furthermore it is far below the national growth rate of gross domestic product. However, there are other factors exacerbating this situation. First is the increasing number of low-paying less-technical jobs. Second is the movement of major American-high paying technical jobs to south of the border. Third is enough emphasis put on the infrastructure that would help the growth of the industrial sector and, hence, the economy (more on this topic in chapter 9). And fourth is the changing economic power structure which is displayed by increasing oligopolies (more on this topic in chapter 5).

A NATION OF HAMBURGER FLIPPERS

In the previous chapter it was stated that relatively fewer high-income-generating jobs are predicted to be created in the first decade of the twenty-first century. Two key factors are primarily responsible for this situation: too much bottom lining and wildly running management pay.

Too much bottom lining is related to the prevailing preoccupation with cost cutting on the part of American industry. Instead of focusing on competitiveness related to an organization's ability to develop core competencies based on its new technologies, skills, experience and knowledge, American firms are just emphasizing cost cutting (Hamel and Prahalad 1994). This orientation is leading primarily in the direction of delayering and downsizing. Many companies that downsize have the focal point of actual reduction of head count. They fail to plan for how to move forward as leaner and meaner organizations. These workforce reductions are traumatic for all parties concerned (Nelson 1997). Companies such as Sears, GM, IBM, and NationsBank have been laying off thousands upon thousands of people. Many of these people, after a while, find jobs paying much less than their previous employment. Additionally, the number of people receiving the minimum wage is growing. Minimum wage, however, has not kept up with economic growth and inflation. In fact its increase has been extremely slow during the course of the past two decades or so.

According to some, one of the reasons for creating fewer high-paying jobs is the move of American industry down south of the border. The adverse impact of NAFTA on Latino and black American jobs resulted in thousands of job losses (Del Olmo 1997). These jobs moved south of the border where wages are much lower.

Finally, the power structure has become so lopsided that while some of the very top executives of the American corporate world are receiving totally exorbitant salaries and other related compensations, the lower levels in those corporate entities are led to believe that they should be grateful that they have a job. If the market system worked properly, an executive's pay would rise when the boss delivers profits to shareholders, and it would fall when the corporate performance declines. In recent years in the American market, it is not working in this textbook fashion. While stockholders' equity and company profitability have remained somewhat stagnant, executive pay has skyrocketed (Reingold and Grover 1999). The highest CEO salary was $575.6 million in 1998, while the average worker pay was $22,976. This situation is leading in the direction of the demise of the American middle class in favor of the very rich and against the poor.

Many mass media critics have been referring to the current American job creation activity as generating a nation of hamburger flippers. Clearly, such service jobs do not make a contribution to the economy as a whole, nor do they provide a job opportunity pasture that will lead to better jobs and greater incomes. In fact, these jobs pay minimum wage, which simply is not adequate to make a reasonable living and raise a family.

Most of these hamburger-flipping-type positions are dead-end jobs. They do not provide any valuable training. They do not open up doors to other jobs and, hence, improvement in worker skills and worker economic well-being does not take place.

Finally, most of these jobs are slightly less than full-time and, therefore, they do not provide Social Security, unemployment and medical care benefits. At the writing of this book, there are estimated to be about 40 million Americans without any medical insurance. At the same time, mass media dwelled upon a study conducted by Tufts University entitled *The Hunger Project*. The study indicated that some 30 million Americans do not know where their next meal will be coming from, and it also estimated that one out of six children are born into poverty. All of these are not necessarily hamburger flippers; however, many are. It can be seen that hamburger-flipping-type jobs are one of the worst ways of utilizing society's human resources. Not only do these individuals lose, but society loses even more. These people with limited means cannot buy much of anything. Potential opportunities for more product and service production are not materialized and, accordingly, markets do not grow.

The economy does not receive advantages of the multiplier effect that would create an upward spiral as better paying jobs are created and the nation's human resources are better utilized. Hence, the loss for the economy is greater than the sum total of all individual losses.

FROM EQUALITY TO EQUAL OPPORTUNITY

Some seventy years of communism in the USSR proved that people are not equal in terms of skills and competence and, therefore, they cannot be equal economically. However, the unique characteristic of a market economy is that it can provide (at least it is supposed to provide) opportunity for each and every individual to advance individually, professionally and economically. However, this unique characteristic of the market economy should not be taken as a given. It is not an automatic outcome of the market economy. In order for every individual to advance according to his or her personal capabilities, there must be equal opportunity for everyone. In the introductory chapter, a brief discussion was presented on equal opportunity. Later on in this book there will be more detailed discussions on the specifics of this concept. Suffice it to say here that if the individual cannot develop the knowledge base for problem-solving and decision-making and the resultant skills for high-quality work-related performance, that individual is not making progress individually and is not making a contribution to society (see chapter 10).

Although economic equality is considered an impossibility, equal opportunity is very much within the scope of capitalism. In other words, everyone in society must have access to education, advice, skill-building, better jobs—in short, to self-advancement. However, once again, the market left alone does not create provisions that are necessary for equal opportunity. The conditions for such a proposition as equal opportunity must be carefully considered and deliberately implemented. Left alone, the market does not provide opportunities for a high-level education in inner cities, does not provide opportunities for the underprivileged to develop skills, does not provide special guidance for those who need it to become better and more productive individuals, does not provide opportunity for physical development and, above all, left to itself, the market does not provide automatically large sums of money to develop the conditions for equal opportunity. Society, both at federal and local levels, must make decisions and a concerted effort to create a total setting of equal opportunity, for all.

However, currently there is no evidence of an emerging aura of equal opportunity. In fact, just the opposite appears prevalent. The merger mania, deteriorating income distribution and declining competition that are mentioned earlier in chapter 1, and all of the activities that are blocking the empowerment of American consumers that are alluded to in the introductory chapter and at the beginning of this chapter, indicate that there is an emerging tyranny of economic power. That power is favoring those who are overprivileged and terrorizing those who are underprivileged. But, in reality, again, American society is the real loser. It is losing income, opportunities to use its manpower, resources, possibilities of making full use of its production facilities.

THE TYRANNY IS REAL

As stated by Kacapyr, Francese and Crispell (1996), at least three-fifths of American households have not seen a real increase in their income during the past ten years. One possible explanation provided by the authors is that people are going deeper into debt. I partially believe that tyranny is being experienced primarily by the American middle class, which is generated by the medical and financial sectors of the American economy. It is this tyranny that is causing much indebtedness and excessive costs without giving an opportunity for the middle class to get ahead economically.

In 1994 Hillary Rodham Clinton tried to initiate a single-payer medical plan for the United States. This was shut down primarily by multi-billion-dollar advertising efforts of insurance companies. The objection to the plan primarily dwelled upon the points that it will provide no choice for patients and it will force individuals to give up their physicians. Some five years later, the prevailing private plans are doing exactly what critics accused the Clinton plan of potentially doing. When companies change medical service providers, workers lose their physicians.

As service providers change, individuals are not quite sure what they are covered for and what they are paying for. In the meantime, insurance companies are taking one-third of all of the medical expenditures off the top without delivering any medical service. Furthermore, they are insuring people selectively—that is, those who can pay and/or those who do not suffer from a previously existing medical condition. There has been a steady increase in the number of the uninsured, estimated to be around 40 million. In the Middle Ages people in the world worried about religious tyranny or military tyranny. In the first half of the twentieth century the world witnessed two major attempts at world conquest by tyrants. However, tyranny does not mean just an evil emperor or a bad king. It can happen if, for instance, the consumer's bank or health-care giver has too much power and if it doesn't have the consumer's well-being in mind, then that consumer can be terrorized.

Let us explore some aspects of this terror that is caused by health-care providers. First and foremost, they are for-profit organizations. Therefore, they try to cut costs. Up to a point, such an orientation has merit, but what providers are doing with their autonomy is pressuring the quality of health care to give way to cost savings. In pursuing cost savings, providers are becoming more and more involved in case management, streamlined referrals and specialized clinics. As a result, patients are spending fewer days in hospitals, and are receiving less service. They also are increasingly treated as numbers. A physician's efficiency is measured with the number of patients he can see within a given period of time, and how much in terms of medical tests and procedures he can generate for the company. All of these measures are leading in the direction of deteriorating medical services and consumer helplessness regarding the services they are receiving and how much they are paying for them. Consumers are not necessarily receiving the service they need because of insurance companies' limitations regarding what the service providers are allowed to do. Some service providers are openly or subtly encouraged to use the largest possible procedures by the insurance companies or health maintenance organizations (HMOs). Thus, consumers are also receiving expensive and sometimes unnecessary procedures. Service providers are teaming up with hospitals directly in order to compete with insurance companies' pressures of cost cutting and competitiveness. In all cases, cost appears to be a much more important focal point than quality.

This general situation is terrorizing consumers because the market system is trying to create entrepreneurs out of doctors and is assuming that this kind of competition is likely to deliver better quality service. However, indications are such that at no time in the history of mankind have people paid so much for so little medical service of questionable quality. It almost automatically brings about the question of whether a single-payer nonprofit system would provide better quality medical care. It appears that the current system is terrorizing the American consumer. Those who are lucky enough to have medical care are exploited by the system. The system is also excluding about 40 million Americans who have no medical care and are poor profit risks, even though they may be as deserving of medical care as any other citizen. Exhibit 2–1 contrasts for-profit multiple payers versus not-for-profit single-payer alternatives. Unlike the single-payer systems of Canada, Great Britain or a number of other countries, U.S. consumers are being pushed around. On paper, a multiple-payer system is likely to create competition and offer more alternatives for consumers; however, the way the current system is working, as illustrated in the exhibit, consumers are being terrorized with no alternatives to extraordinary expenses and very mediocre service. The question, therefore, is should there not be a single-payer such as in the British or Canadian systems? Although government bureaucracies are not considered very efficient, the totally fractured private medical market, full of non-service-giving insurance companies that are collecting very high premiums, is not likely to be efficient either. (Please see Appendix A to this chapter for an individual experience with an HMO.)

WHAT ABOUT THE BANKING SECTOR?

Another example of American consumers being terrorized can be seen in the banking sector, which, as it continues its merger mania, is becoming further and further removed from consumers and their particular needs. Whereas consumers need institutions to help them solve their financial problems, they are facing institutions who just loan money and take the attitude that consumers should be grateful since they were able to borrow.

American banks are using consumers' money, paying almost nothing for its use. They are charging exorbitant rates of interest for consumers to use their own money. Furthermore, banks are charging a variety of fees on top of the interest they charge for consumers to use *their own* money.

Exhibit 2–1
Some of the Key Differences Between Profit and Nonprofit Medical Care

Medical Care Delivery For Profit (Multiple Payer)	Medical Delivery Nonprofit (Single Payer)
Using most expensive procedures	Using procedures that are just right
Requiring more than necessary procedures	Not requiring more than necessary procedures
Doctors are forced to see more and more patients	Doctors see fewer patients and provide more quality time
Medical caregivers are merging patients are forced to change doctors	Patients do not need to change their doctors
Insurance companies for lower cost medical caregivers hire new doctors to replace more expensive old ones. Patients are forced to change doctors	Patients do not need to change their doctors, they stay with their doctors for long periods
Insurance companies constantly change their approved caregiver list making it impossible for patients to make "good" decisions	Patients do not have difficulty staying with the same specialists, or having an opportunity to see any specialist they need to
Cost is preferred over quality	Quality is preferred over cost

While banks are charging about 12 percent plus initiation fees for a personal loan, they are paying less than 1 percent for checking accounts. This is an incredible discrepancy stemming from diminishing competition in the banking sector. (Please see Appendix B for an individual experience with a bank.)

These two industries, medical care and banking, indicate how consumers are facing situations where their options and their power are being chipped away. As was briefly discussed in the introductory chapter and in this chapter,

American consumers are losing ground as businesses become larger and more powerful, not necessarily because of their merits as businesses, but because of the brute power they are acquiring through merger mania. As this mania continues, more and more attention is paid to the bottom line and more and more cost cutting is occurring in place of quality in services or products. Simultaneously, however, Americans are losing ground as they are laid off from their jobs and, because of this *bottom lining*, cannot find equally good jobs afterward.

DOWNSIZING IS NOT RIGHT SIZING

During the past two decades, along with merger mania, there has been an accelerating movement that is referred to as "downsizing" by its critics and "right sizing" by its proponents. At least two specific reasons can account for this acceleration. These have nothing to do with a firm's being more competitive or performing well in the marketplace. First, companies lay off people up front to look lean and be attractive for a merger or takeover; second, top managements, in the short run, by laying off parts of middle management, look good and justify very large raises and bonuses.

Simultaneously, however, new cross-disciplinary concepts have emerged to challenge traditional marketing thought and business practices. Among these, two are critical in terms of downsizing: "lean thinking" and the "lean enterprise" (Morgan and Piercy 1996). These two emerging concepts rationally justify the downsizing concept. The idea, of course, is to make certain people work harder and reduce the number of workers in the organization. Lean thinking in some people's minds is equated with efficiency. But when the firm lays off many people, which is primarily done by the personnel division and not by strategic planning groups in the company, it is often caught off base regarding its core competencies. The people who are laid off may have and often are representing the firm's core competencies that justify its existence. In other words, the firm loses its competitiveness as excessive downsizing activity sets in. Thus, there is a fine line between downsizing and lean thinking.

The impact of downsizing on the individual in our society is profound. Not being able to find similar or better jobs and being forced to accept an inferior position is a waste of human resources in society. Unfortunately our economic system or our accounting procedures do not have a way to track down these huge wastes of human resources. Additionally, however, young workers see this situation as not having opportunities for advancement; therefore, there is not much to look forward to. They see the situation as being forced to look for other jobs before they are laid off by the company. Similarly, if young talent does not go through this stage of progression, it is not clear how society will train its future leaders. In other words, if talented young workers do not get promotions and do not advance within the organizational hierarchy, they will not become mature enough to assume leadership positions within society. Thus, from many different perspectives, downsizing cannot be a very useful concept and should not be coined as "right sizing."

With downsizing, along with other forces that are eliminating good paying and challenging jobs that are likely to train future leaders of society, the cost of living based on diminishing competition and merger mania is going up. An estimated 60 percent of housewives are working, and two-paycheck families are still barely making ends meet. Similarly, as discussed earlier, the income generated by society is distributed in a very uneven manner in such a way that those who are very rich are getting much richer, while many of those who are middle class are becoming poor. Somehow, the mighty American economy must be able to create more and better opportunities, especially for those who are not able to get ahead. It must be recognized that if the economic base becomes larger, everybody in society gets richer. Hence, those who are in a position to create opportunities for those who are not able to get ahead on their own will be benefiting themselves.

CREATING OPPORTUNITIES

Constant cost cutting and bottom lining are not orientations that are likely to create good paying jobs that lead to greater economic riches. American enterprises are not in the cost-cutting business, they are in the business of wealth generation (Drucker 1999). Creating opportunities in the economy calls for deliberate action and proactive behavior. This proactivity, regardless if it is within or without the constraints of the public sector, implies challenging the existing laissez-faire ("lazy fare," as one of my friends used to call it), orientation. Instead, some parameters by both the private and public sectors should be established to stimulate the economy further and to distribute its gains more equitably. As mentioned earlier, top executive pay in the corporate world has gone completely out of control, with some executives making $300 million or more a year. There are no limits to their pay. However, there is a limit for a minimum wage that is received by millions, and that has very stringent limits. Certainly such conditions do not indicate the presence of some degree of equity.

The market, as was stated earlier, only reacts; it does not plan or establish parameters for economic progress. Therefore, it does not automatically take corrective action if the conditions worsen. It took Franklin D. Roosevelt a number of years to counteract the Great Depression and to reverse it. This was accomplished by numerous new job-creating projects and investment programs. None of these would have taken place if the market was left alone to continue the way it was. There was a need for proactive projects.

Being proactive in this case implies, first and foremost, understanding that all investments do not contribute evenly to economic growth. An investment in the automotive industry in Detroit may create proportionately more jobs and more income than investing the same amount in the same industry in Silicon Valley. Contrariwise, investing in the computer industry in Silicon Valley may create many more jobs and more income than the same investment would generate in Detroit. Similarly, there are industries that will create more and better jobs in the economy and, as a result, they will create greater economic development. As considered in macro economics, the economic multiplier is greater for some industries in the country as a whole but may be even greater in certain regions. More is presented on this topic in chapter 9. However, it must be reiterated that at this point in time, this is not quite happening. Industries are not expanding, and high-paying jobs are not being created. At this time, the truly booming component of the American economy is the stock market, which is a further indication of the divisiveness of the market system. Those who have a lot of money are making much more in the stock market, whereas those who do not have much money are left behind. Clearly, this situation is generating a greater gap between the rich and the poor in the American market that is totally contrary to the empowerment of the American consumer.

SUMMARY

This chapter explores the plight of the American consumer from a macro perspective. It makes a very serious point about the American market's being divided into "rich" and "poor" markets. It projects a grim picture of an America which will increasingly be composed of hamburger flippers if nothing is done about the deepening trends. Brute economic power, caused by endless merger mania driven not by benefiting consumers but by sheer greed, is creating a tyranny for the American consumer. In order to show how helpless the American consumer is when facing this tyranny, reference is made to the banking industry and the health-care industry.

As merger mania continues, downsizing and the creation of ineffective gigantic corporations also continue. Thus, more and more American families need two paychecks to make ends meet. One major countermeasure is to generate economic growth and resultant good-paying jobs. It is maintained here that in order to succeed in such an activity, the private and public sectors must cooperate and generate a proactive and orderly progressing economic growth. However, as illustrated in Appendixes A and B, consumers are being squeezed from many directions, and there does not seem to be any relief in sight.

REFERENCES

Del Olmo, Frank (1997). "Support For NAFTA Is Unraveling," *Los Angeles Times*, 116, August 3.

Drucker, Peter F. (1999). *Management Challenges for the 21st Century*. New York: HarperBusiness.

Hamel, G. and Prahalad, C. K. (1994). *Competing for the Future*. Boston: Harvard Business School Press.

Kacapyr, Elia; Francese, Peter; and Crispell, Diana (1996). "Are You Middle Class 2?" *American Demographics*, 18, October, 30–36.

Leonhardt, David (1997). "Two-Tier Marketing," *Business Week*, March 17, 82–90.

Morgan, Neil A. and Piercy, Nigel F. (1996). "Competitive Advantage, Quality Strategy and the Role of Marketing," *British Journal of Management*, 7, 231–245.

Nelson, Bob (1997). "The Care of Un-downsized," *Training and Development*, 51, April, 40–44.

Reingold, Jennifer and Grover, Ronald (1999). "Is Greed Good?" *Business Week*, April 19, 85–99.

Samli, A. Coskun (1993). *Counterturbulence Marketing*. Westport, CT: Quorum Books.

APPENDIX A: MY HMO IS TELLING ME NOT TO GET SICK OR ELSE

Some years ago when Hillary Rodham Clinton came up with a very challenging and comprehensive medical report, insurance companies spent billions for its defeat. They mainly claimed that no one will be able to choose their doctor or stay with them. Well! guess what, during the past six years I had to change doctors about five times. The first one disappeared. The second one was not very good. The third one retired. The fourth one was changed by the insurance company and finally, I found out that my current doctor is quitting his practice. Is this what we were promised? I hardly have a choice in this matter. By the way, the doctor must be in the approved provider list OR ELSE.

In the history of mankind never have so many people paid so much for so little. This statement can describe our medical system as it stands today. Over 40 million Americans don't have any medical coverage and the rest don't quite know what they have coverage for. However, they are paying dearly for that unclear coverage. And more than 75 percent are asking for an overhaul. Although we have the best medical system in the world in terms of knowledge, it is totally inadequate in terms of delivery. Many third world countries have better delivery systems.

Medical care for Americans is totally controlled by cost rather than the needed medical attention. Although Americans are paying twice as much as Canadians and three times as much as the British, the dissatisfaction rate in the United States is substantially greater than these two countries.

When you have to go to a specialist you need a referral. If you need to go to the hospital you need a referral. If the insurance does not approve the procedure or the medical attention you need, you are out of luck. If your doctor is not in the approved service provider's list, again you are out of luck. The decision is not made by your doctor but by your insurance company. Insurance companies who are not delivering any medical service are taking out about 30 percent of all of the medical expenditures and telling both doctors and patients what to do! All of this is done in the name of "free enterprise" and the market system. As things get worse I feel funny in my classes talking about the market economy and consumer orientation that makes the market economy very strong.

The free market system, in the absence of some checks and balances or outside controls by some authority who is taking the consumers' well-being as a higher priority than cost controls, is certainly giving way to tyranny. Cost controls have gone to such extremes that if there are new medications or new treatments for your ailment you cannot use them because they are not approved. There is no justification for the insurance industry to call the shots just because some people do not believe in a single-payer system. Why can't we have some variation of the British two-tier system. In the first tier everyone is covered for by a single payer. The second tier is free selection of doctors, medication and treatment in a privatized manner. In the United States the two political parties are so involved in an ideological battle that they are not getting anything done. In the meantime, millions of Americans are experiencing a tyranny that is not exercised by an evil empire but by an evil insurance system that has no business being between the doctors and patients.

APPENDIX B: MY BANK IS TERRORIZING ME

Tyranny does not necessarily mean an evil king or an evil empire pushing the citizens around. It can happen that a private institution—your bank, your HMO, or your insurance company, among others—can easily do the same kinds of things that the evil empire could do and terrorize you. I know you will say, how can that be? There is competition and if, say, the bank does not function properly, you can go to another bank. Well, the theory in its textbook version is correct, but pray tell, can you really distinguish Bank A from Bank B? What competition? The old adage, "If you cannot lick them, you join them," has been replaced by "If you cannot lick them, you *buy* them." There is more merger activity in the banking sector than exploration of "How can we serve our customers?" This is a disastrous commentary for a *service* sector.

Just what is happening? I remember during the hot debates of deregulation, we were told that when the banking sector is deregulated, there will be so much competition that consumers will truly benefit from it. Let us examine the record.

I somehow let my checking account go below a large sum. One month I realized that my bank was charging me exorbitant fees because the account had gone below $10,000.00. I paid a visit to the bank and told them that I had no idea that I had to maintain a balance of $10,000.00. Then I asked just how much interest would I receive if I had a $10,000.00 balance. I was told that it would be about 1.8%. I asked what would be the next category. I was told that with a $1,000.00 balance, I would get 1.2%. I then said, "You mean to say that for my $9,000.00, I receive an interest of .6%?" And to my surprise, my not-so-friendly banker said *yes*. But she added if I pay $80.00 a year, I could be put into a higher paying account. I said, "let me understand this. You are charging me to use *my* money, you are hardly paying me any interest, you are penalizing me for not maintaining a $10,000.00 balance and now you are telling me that I have to pay you more to receive a higher level of interest?" I felt I was being terrorized.

Unfortunately, with the same bank, I had a simple run-in. I had to send some money from my bank to the same bank in a different city. My party was waiting there. My bank told me that it would take about forty-eight hours. I said I would pay for the long-distance call and to please call the specific teller and authorize giving my party a check. I do not see how this could take more than fifteen minutes. To make a long story longer, after arguing a few hours, we managed to get the money in about four hours total. Needless to say, I was charged an arm and a leg for fees that I did not know even existed.

Recently, two small checks from my tenant in a rental property I own were bounced. My bank charged *me* a penalty. Now mind you, I still have a lot of money in my checking account, and the bank is using that money very freely. When I told them that it was not my fault, they told me that it was not their fault either. But still, I am the one who is being terrorized.

My mortgage payments with the same bank are always on time, except when the Post Office somehow did not deliver one (or better yet, it was lost by an inept person, who should not handle my account). Certainly, I was told that I should stop payment on the old check and write a new one. Guess what the fee for stopping payments is? So large that I decided to take a chance with the old check. My mortgage payments never pass the deadlines, but invariably every month I get a threatening letter from the all-knowing computer that my payment is late, but if it is in the mail, forget this note. Constant harassment, as shown, is the standard procedure.

Now, I am a very busy person. In the past, I did most of my banking on Saturdays. One day I learned that my bank will no longer be open on Saturdays. I was told that it was not cost-effective (or did they say, it is interfering with their Saturday morning golfing?).

In the meantime, I just learned that the interest I am receiving has gone down to .7 of 1%. (I was not even told that the interest rates are variable.) But then, my bank, by using my $10,000.00, is making at least $1,200.00, of which I am getting $70.00. Wow, deregulation and free market are really helping! If the consumer is the *king*, I certainly feel dethroned. I am being terrorized. Can I just deal with cash and avoid the banks? I do not even have that choice.

Chapter 3

Equal Opportunity Consumer

In a democratic society, individuals have equal legal rights. This is a key tenet of democracy. Individuals are not discriminated against, and in the eyes of the law all citizens are equal. Such concepts are promoted so that a false impression can be formulated regarding consumers. Persons against government intervention would lead us to believe that left alone and free of government intervention, American consumers have equal opportunity. This certainly is not the case.

In a market economy, consumers must have equal opportunity. Within the constraints of their capabilities, they perhaps will fulfill their goals. Therefore, no two persons are likely to be exactly alike, or are expected to act alike, but all consumers are to be given the same opportunity to pursue their own social and economic activities leading to their own happiness.

Biologically and genetically, consumers are not equal, and it is likely that they will never be equal. But this does not preclude having equal opportunity. In the previous chapter, the plight of the American consumer is discussed. It is stated that the market is imposing on individuals different types of pressures at different levels. In this chapter, an attempt is made to point out how this plight is exacerbated with the lack of equal capability to absorb, react or perform. Based on the individual consumer's characteristics (or frailties), the externally generated plight can become almost totally impossible to cope with. Hence to have an "equal opportunity consumer" in the American economy becomes a more and more remote possibly.

It must be strongly asserted that equal opportunity for consumers will enable not only consumers to advance as far as they can but also society as a whole. If the citizens of a society can develop their capabilities, skills and talents as much as they can, society advances as well, because it is utilizing its human resources as much as possible and as effectively as possible.

WHAT DO AMERICAN CONSUMERS NEED?

Just like all consumers anywhere in the world, American consumers' needs can be summarized in terms of three key areas: security, income and opportunity. There are many other considerations and factors, but these three are particularly critical in maintaining continuity in the economy and providing equity for the consumer. These are the fundamentals in empowering the consumer.

Security: consumers' security is related to having a job and making sure that the job will be there tomorrow. This kind of assurance can be partially measured by the "index of consumer confidence" published by the University of Michigan. This particular measure determines the general state of mind of American consumers. Having a high level of confidence in the economy and in the short run provides important continuity for the economy and the markets. After all, if consumers do not expect major disruptions in their economic well-being, then they will be able to continue their lifestyles and routines. This, by definition, maintains the level of stability that is needed for consumers to employ their purchasing power in a fully empowered manner.

Income: without adequate income, consumers cannot participate in the market. They cannot buy products and services that would enhance their quality of life. This income must be enjoying a reasonable level of expected increase so that consumers will have an optimistic approach to their lives and their consumption patterns. Expected modest increases in incomes provide opportunities to plan improvements in consumer lifestyles.

Opportunity: for consumers, opportunity implies having access to goods and services, including education, medical care and entertainment to name a few. If consumers do not have reasonably equal access to these, they cannot possibly achieve and maintain a desirable quality of life. Thus, they cannot be identified as "empowered."

Consider, for instance, Mrs. X, who is partially on public assistance. She is physically handicapped because of a job-related accident many years ago. She is also a single mother and has a very intelligent, young preteen son. If Mrs. X does not have access to good education, her son will not have the opportunity to cultivate his natural intelligence; but above all, society will miss out by not using its human resources effectively.

It is critical to realize that many points discussed in chapter 2 are not likely to allow the possibility of having equal opportunity for consumers in the American economy. In fact, it was posited that there is a continuing development in the direction of increasing economic inequalities. If we add internal inequalities on top of economic inequalities, it becomes obvious that the equal opportunity consumer is simply a myth. In the eyes of the legal system, all individuals are equal, but in the marketplace American consumers are not at all equal. Exhibit 3–1 illustrates four key forces that make it difficult for consumers to have equal opportunity without considering their personal biological and psychological characteristics.

1. Monopolized power, by definition, reduces consumers' potential equal opportunity, since it distorts income distribution and hence individuals' capability to reach out and receive the best education, the best medical care, the best skills and so forth.

2. Increasing complexity of the society, again by definition, creates unequal opportunities as well as problems for the consumer. As will be discussed in the next chapter, increasing complexity of the society makes it difficult for people with somewhat limited mental and educational capabilities to respond easily and proficiently.

3. The availability of information or lack of it makes the complexity issue more serious. The inadequacy of information makes it difficult for consumers to make good decisions and enjoy opportunities as they eliminate problems. Although the information may be there, but for some with limited capabilities, it may not be retrievable.

4. Inequitable distribution of income limits consumers' opportunity to buy, to use or to consume all the goods and services the society has to offer. By definition, this situation limits individuals' quality of life.

INNATE INEQUALITIES OF THE CONSUMER

Although it is different in legal terms, biologically all people are not born equal. On the contrary, all people are unequal in that everyone is unique. Some people are brilliant, some people are adequate and some others are rather slow. Some people are more frail as consumers than others. All con-

Exhibit 3–1
The Myth of the Equal Opportunity Consumer

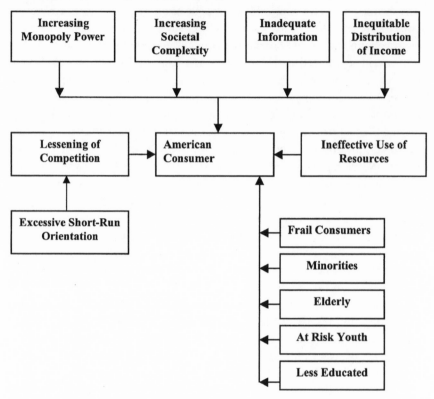

Source: Adapted and revised from Samli (1992).

sumers, therefore, cannot cope with the rapidly changing economic conditions and constantly increasing complexities of society. Those who are very bright may be ahead of the changes and may even use the increasing complexities to their advantage. Bill Gates created a spectacular company based on advances in the computer and software industries. But there are also millions who cannot use the computer or even understand just what it does.

CONSUMERS' WELL BEING: THE RECENT PAST

When John F. Kennedy introduced what is now known as the consumer manifesto, he posited that society is much too complex for the old concept of caveat emptor (let the buyer beware), which was, and to a certain extent is, the general practice in the American market system. Up to that point, consumers were responsible to protect themselves and make wise purchase and consumption decisions.

Kennedy's assertions made some impact in the direction of moving from caveat emptor to caveat vendor (let the seller beware). Kennedy wanted to accomplish caveat vendor by proposing four major rights for the consumer: (1) the right to know, (2) the right to choose, (3) the right to be protected, and (4) the right to be heard (Kennedy 1963). These four rights established the foundation of modern American consumerism to protect the consumers and their rights, and emerged as an important movement in our society (Samli 1992). However, in recent years we have witnessed an erosion rather than a reinforcement of this movement. As living in our society becomes more complicated, consumers appear to be more neglected than helped.

As has been discussed in chapters 1 and 2, since consumers' relative economic power is dissipating, and economic adversities are emerging, the American consumerism movement and the closely related caveat vendor concept have both failed.

Since empowerment of the consumer is a power play, the four Kennedy freedoms could not hold as the corporate entity became more and more powerful in the American market system. Consider the following four points. Each is connected to the four Kennedy rights in the same order they were stated above.

- Dow Chemical *concealed* the research results regarding silicone breast implants from the American public. Similarly, the tobacco industry blocked the research findings indicating that nicotine is a highly addictive substance from reaching the American markets. Thus, the right to know is violated in many ways and many times.

- As medical service providers, banks, communications giants and others merge, consumer choice is reduced. Thus, the second proposition in the consumer manifesto is violated.

- As the power of corporate entities increases and as the pressure to deregulate becomes more prominent, consumers' rights to be protected disappear. Fewer laws with lesser power regarding, for instance, the atmosphere in terms of clean air and clean water, reduces consumer protection. The tendency during the past decade or so has been to relax or eliminate many of the existing laws, rather than passing more stringent laws to protect the American consumer.

- As this book is being written, "the patients' bill of rights" which enabled consumers to sue their healthcare providers was voted down in Congress. As the corporate entity gains more power and lawsuits become more expensive, the legal recourse of the Kennedy manifesto is dissipating at a fast pace. In other words, consumers have less and less opportunity to be heard.

As can be seen from these examples, the external conditions are moving in the direction of nonequal opportunity for American consumers. If these external conditions are assessed on the basis of consumers' varying inner capabilities, then the picture becomes even more blurred and more negative.

CONSUMERS' INNER CAPABILITIES

Just as consumers are not equal because of changing external conditions, they are even less equal on the basis of their socioeconomic, psychological and biological makeup. Exhibit 3–1 identifies five at-risk consumer groups. The critical consideration here is consumer competency—in other words, how competent consumers are in spending their funds effectively and making reasonable purchase decisions. Consumer competency is considered much less than necessary for at-risk consumer groups. The lack of competency in these groups occurs to varying degrees. The five at-risk groups considered here are estimated to account for the majority of American society: (1) frail consumers, (2) minorities, (3) the elderly, (4) at-risk youth, and (5) the less educated. Within each group there are still varying degrees of competency.

Frail consumers is the largest of these five groups. Although all five groups can easily be considered as being composed of frail consumers, in this section, a more stringent definition is utilized. Since the average intelligence is about 100 IQ points, just about half of the population may be considered slightly or somewhat seriously below that level. In a complex society with a multitude of products and consumer decision situations, some of these people can be considered frail in the sense that they will have a difficult time making good purchase decisions of goods and services. This group of consumers, depending upon mental capabilities and degree of independence, would need much help to achieve some degree of consumer competence and to reach an approximation of equal opportunity.

Minorities, mainly immigrants, are quite frail, particularly if they are lacking English-language skills and are not physically mobile. Because they may not have a vehicle in which to shop around and because they may not have English proficiency, they may not be able to comparison shop and may be discriminated against by their compatriots who are less than totally honest and who manage stores in special neighborhoods. Many years ago a number of studies indicated that such practices are rather commonplace in major cities such as Los Angeles, New York or Chicago.

The elderly comprise the fastest growing sector in the American market. They also have limited mobility. Therefore, they also are dependent on local stores and their personnel. Additionally, the elderly have special needs in terms of care, medication and human interaction. These needs are, in some cases, very strong, and these consumers' dependency on these can make them rather frail. They have little, if any, bargaining power, and they have limited economic means. Therefore, their level of dependency on service providers makes them quite vulnerable.

At-risk youth, by definition, have little competency as consumers. They are very much under peer pressure, they have limited information coming from rather unreliable sources such as MTV and they buy impulsively. They are extremely fad prone and fashion influenced. As a result of all of these (and perhaps many more) weaknesses indicating less-than-adequate competencies, this group is particularly frail. They are the ones who believe that if they buy Nike shoes they may play basketball just like Michael Jordan.

Finally, different estimates indicate that about 25 percent of Americans are functionally illiterate. They cannot read or write well enough to get a job and maintain it. As consumers, they certainly cannot take advantage of good prices, nor can they read the small print in contractual agreements. They cannot, in certain circumstances, even find the location where there may be menial jobs available that do not require some degree of literacy.

These five groups have some similarities and many differences. However, each may indicate a certain type of consumer frailty which is considered here to be a stronger and more dangerous concept than overall consumer incompetence. It may be stated that all frail consumers are incompetent, but not all incompetent consumers are frail.

Perhaps the most important point to be considered here is the fact that both frailty and incompetency are self-perpetuating. Unless something is done to rectify consumer incompetency or smooth out the negative impact of consumer frailty, the equal opportunity consumer concept will remain a myth in American society.

Blanchard, Carlos and Randolph (1996) make a very critical point as they discuss empowerment. Their position is that empowerment is not magic. It is just some simple ideas and a lot of smart work that must begin at the top, and it certainly takes a long time. Just dealing with one aspect of consumer empowerment, elimination of self-perpetuating consumer frailty, is rather complicated and must start from the top. The top here is the state or federal government. Because this is a very costly social affliction, self-perpetuation of consumer frailty must be taken very seriously. In no way could it correct itself without help from both private and public power structures.

SELF-PERPETUATION OF CONSUMER FRAILTY

Frail consumers, besides being inadequately literate, poor and sometimes mentally somewhat less than average, are underprivileged in that there is no adequate information, reasonable education or at least some legal protection available to ease off the pressures of consumer decision-making. Such consumers do not have the capabilities to make good decisions regarding the identification of their own needs, prioritizing them, searching for information, comparing alternatives and finally purchasing the most appropriate goods and services according to needs, budget and reason (Kotler 1997).

The frail consumer's ability to make good economic decisions is also hampered by the ability to reasonably identify and assess the risks involved in many purchase transactions. Somewhat limited mental capability can easily distort the perception of potential risks in directions of plus or minus. In other words, the risk may be exaggerated or understated, one way or the other.

Distorted risk perception is likely to lead to suboptimized purchase decisions, less-than-adequate purchases and inadequate use of the individual's economic resources. Samli, Sirgy, and Lederhaus (1992) refer to this complex situation as "distorted risk management" by certain individual consumers. The position they have taken can be described by the following quotation (p. 70):

> The core assumption in classical economics is that the consumer is an all-knowing and calculating creature who attempts to maximize utilities in purchasing. . . . However, . . . individuals are differently endowed and may not necessarily maximize utilities in their purchases.

They go on to state that frail consumers are those people who not only cannot optimize purchase satisfaction, but also, because of their distorted risk management, become even more underprivileged. In some ways, such distorted risk management can even be dangerous in terms of buying the wrong product and using it inappropriately. Risks run the gamut from a simple but reasonably common practice of drinking diet drinks between meals or buying risky toys for children, to more serious activities such as not coordinating the medication one may be taking or not understanding the details when one buys health insurance. In other words frail consumers' risks vary from very serious to not so serious. However, in all cases they are costly and contrary to consumer empowerment.

Exhibit 3–2 indicates that consumer frailty, uninterrupted, is self-perpetuating. It reinforces itself. Whether or not, unchecked, it gets worse is an issue that is not known and that must be carefully investigated. It is also necessary to explore the total social cost of frail consumers' making less-than-optimal consumption decisions. If they are not making good decisions and perhaps endangering themselves or by buying the wrong things and wasting their limited budgets, they are cornering themselves in such a way that they are becoming in greater need of public assistance.

CORRECTIVE ACTION IS NECESSARY

Samli (1992) posits three different forms of corrective action to reduce or eliminate self-perpetuating frailty: consumer information, consumer education and consumer protection. These are all very involved topics, discussed just briefly here.

Consumer Information

There are many different ways of making adequate consumer information available so that consumers can make better purchase and consumption decisions. Advertising, if it is quite factual, is very effective because of its far reach in society.

Labels that are attached to products are very critical. They provide information regarding the contents of the product, how it must be used and cared for and so forth. There may be other special instructions that come with the product, perhaps as an attachment to the package or container.

Similarly, warning signs or information about the dangers of the product are made available. Some drugstores now automatically examine the compatibility of numerous medications if the consumer is taking them simultaneously. Finally, there may be special brochures or flyers regarding the product in question. These will give more detailed information about the product and its features.

Consumer Education

Consumer education comes in two major forms, formal and informal. Formal consumer education is composed of university or college courses, such as consumer economics or consumer finance which are very important in

Exhibit 3–2
Self-Perpetuating Consumer Frailty

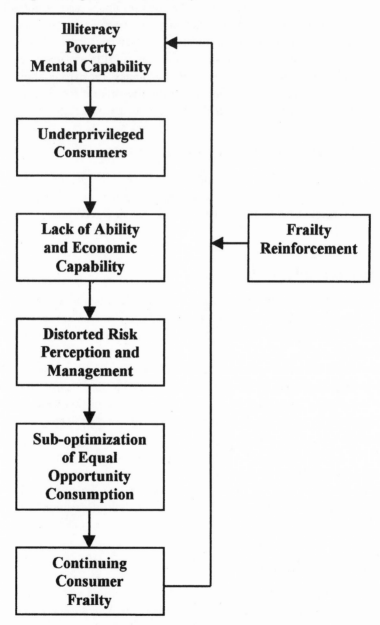

Source: Adapted and revised from Samli (1992).

terms of providing direction for better consumer decision-making. Special courses in health care, nutrition, exercise, home management and personal finance are all designed to accomplish the same goal: creating an educated consumer. A better educated consumer is more likely to avoid distorted risk perception and, to a substantial extent, overcome frailty.

There are also many informal options relating to consumer education. Numerous conferences, workshops, seminars, lectures and continuing education types of courses are extremely beneficial. Perhaps the most important consideration in the consumer education area is making sure that frail consumers are guided to utilize these opportunities and benefit from this array of options. With the advance of computer usage and the Internet, consumer education options are likely to be increased. Individuals will be able to get necessary information from the Internet at their convenience.

Consumer Protection

America is a land of contrasts and contradictions. It is curious that our society is depicted as a country of laws and yet many attempts are made to deregulate. Consumer protection first and foremost is related to generating laws and enforcing them so that those who cannot cope with ever-increasing complexities of our society can improve their decision-making patterns. Consumer protection can vary from banning certain products, such as Red Dye No. 2, to specifying certain trade practices, such as truth in lending or bait and switch in retailing. Having offices of consumer affairs and investigating consumer complaints is a critical consideration in the same direction. Consumers must have opportunities to raise their opinions, complaints, needs or concerns.

Traditionally there have been government agencies to oversee consumer protection and safety. The Federal Trade Commission, the Product Safety Commission, the Food and Drug Administration and the Office of Consumer Affairs are to name just a few. All of these and many others are an attempt to help primarily the frail consumers protect themselves against questionable products and services. However, in recent years, both political parties, particularly the Republicans, have been very outspoken about deregulation. As a result, many of these organizations do not have as much power as they used to, and it appears that they are catering to *corporate whims* rather than to *consumer needs*. It is unfortunate that corporate whims are going against consumer needs in such areas as the Dalkon shield, intrauterine devices that caused cancer, research on the dangers of silicone breast implants and research reports indicating that nicotine is one of the most addictive substances.

If, despite increased need for consumer protection, corporate whims are favored over consumer needs, then there will be less and less protection for American consumers. This situation cannot but exacerbate the dilemma of frail consumers. By not receiving good information and by not having legal recourse and/or protection, frail consumers' consumption and purchase problems are likely to become more noticeable and less and less beneficial to individual consumers (Samli 1992). Consumers in general and relatively more frail consumers in particular cannot claim to be living in a society where there are equal opportunities for consumers.

LIP SERVICE FOR CAVEAT VENDOR

At the writing of this book, Congress and the tobacco industry are at odds. The industry is making a lot of money by targeting the country's youth and making them addicted to nicotine, but is not willing to stop advertising to young kids and to start carrying some of the burden of medical costs. It appears that the taxpayers are carrying the burden of lung diseases and other related ailments that are afflicting cigarette smokers.

Here, once again, the emphasis is let the buyer beware (caveat emptor). But during the past three decades, American society is supposedly trying to emphasize the let-the-seller-beware mentality, which is much more appropriate in light of the increasing complexities of living and also the increasing numbers of consumers who are at risk. By examining the tobacco case, which is just one of many, it is obvious that instead of making a real effort to help those consumers to become more capable to exercise equal opportunity, American society is paying only lip service to caveat vendor. The sellers with their short-term mentality are not much interested in consumers' well-being. Thus, both parties as well as the society are losing in the long run.

SUMMARY

Consumers, in general, need security, income and opportunity. The prevailing conditions in American markets indicate that these are not made available to average consumers. External conditions are becoming more adverse regarding these needs. But, on the other side of the coin, consumers are not equal in terms of their information, education and capabilities to learn and make reasonable decisions. Some consumers are not quite competent and others are even more frail, since they have more difficulty coping with the constantly increasing complexities of our society.

All consumers, but particularly those who are less competent and more frail, need information, education and protection. This chapter presents a brief discussion of what is available in these areas and what is needed for these three remedial measures so that the American consumer can enjoy a positive movement in the direction of equal opportunity. Unless the internal and external conditions work in the direction of creating competent consumers, no progress can be expected. Thus, the goal must be enhancing consumer competency through consumer education, consumer information and consumer protection. Until the goal of enhancing consumer competency is achieved, equal opportunity consumer is simply a *myth*.

REFERENCES

Blanchard, Ken; Carlos, John P.; and Randolph, Alan (1996). *Empowerment Takes More Than a Minute*. San Francisco: Berrett-Koehler Publishers.

Kennedy, John F. (1993). "Consumer Advisory Council: First Report." Executive Office of the President. Washington DC: U.S. Government Printing Office, October.

Kotler, Philip (1997). *Marketing Management*. Englewood Cliffs, NJ: Prentice-Hall.

Samli, A. Coskun; Sirgy, M. Joseph; and Lederhaus, Mary Ann (1992). "Distorted Risk Management as it Affects Underprivileged Consumers." In A. Coskun Samli, *Social Responsibility in Marketing*. Westport, CT: Quorum Books.

Samli, A. Coskun (1992). *Social Responsibility in Marketing*. Westport, CT: Quorum Books.

Chapter 4

What Complexity Begets Is More Complexity

We live in a very complex society. Republicans, Libertarians and others with similar ways of thinking constantly talk about getting rid of big government. But how big is this big government? And how much should it shrink (if at all)? There are no proper criteria established as to the ideal size of government. However, if we consider the high crime rate, excessive pollution, lack of health insurance for at least 40 million Americans, the ever-increasing number of street people, inadequate education, deteriorating highways and bridges and the like, there needs to be an ever-growing government. While the population is growing arithmetically, society's complexity level is increasing geometrically. It is this ever-growing complexity that creates the need for an ever-growing government.

Of course, the complex problems that American consumers are facing in their daily lives cannot be resolved by simplistic measures. An example of this is the current status of the American income tax code. Politicians constantly talk about making the tax system fairer and more simple. However, fairness and simplicity are totally opposing concepts in most political issues, but particularly in regard to taxation. The more simplistic the tax code, the greater its sweeping discriminations toward certain groups, mainly the poor and those who have limited or fixed incomes. The American tax code is extremely complex because it tries to be fair to all. A flat tax, for example, which is being proposed at the writing of this book, is very regressive and will hurt most consumers, while being a true boon for the upper 1 percent or so of extremely rich Americans.

American society is in a constant change mode. Just consider the revolution that computers have created in our society since the early 1980s. Champion (1988) comments on this "technochange" which is leading to "technostress." She identifies some of the symptoms of technostress as: fear of losing autonomy; fear of losing promotion opportunities; fear of losing control over work environment; fear of social isolation; fear of change; fear of loss of freedom, privacy, and control; fear that technology will increase illiteracy and the like. More recently, McConnell (1996) posited that today's versatile computers have impacted almost all occupations and industries. She went on to say that the computer has launched the information highway and created a whole new market segment—the home market. High-powered computers at home are changing the way the average consumer used to conduct daily business. Thus, computers are transforming the American economy. They are changing the composition and distribution of labor, improving labor efficiency, creating new markets and new forms of organizations.

But computers are only one of the complexity factors. The complexities of the American market can be detected in areas of environmental problems, high crime, large numbers of homeless, medical care, the elderly and the like. All of these are due to increasing complexities of the economy. Left alone, the economy does not resolve these problems, because the market does not plan or prioritize; it simply reacts. In order to understand the changes in the market system and track down its increasing complexities, it is necessary to contrast Adam Smith's market system with the current American market.

FROM ADAM SMITH'S MARKET TO BILL CLINTON'S MARKET

Exhibit 4–1 illustrates the transition from Adam Smith's simple market to the current extremely complex American market. The two markets are compared on the basis of seven different factors. The changes are interpreted in terms of their impact on American consumers.

In Adam Smith's market, enterprises were numerous and very small. One particular business could not make a special impact in the market and create a strong reaction or a ripple effect in terms of changing the way business was conducted. In Clinton's market, this whole picture is reversed. There

Exhibit 4–1
A Comparison of Adam Smith's Market to Bill Clinton's Current Market

Comparison Factors	Adam Smith's Market	Clinton's Current Market	Critical Consumer Impact
Enterprises	Numerous and very small	Relatively fewer and many are too big	Limiting consumer choice and negotiation power
Business Decision Areas	Rather simple, dealing with some basic decisions	Multitudinous, complex and dealing with multiple decisions	Removed from the consumer
Information	Limited need but fully available both to business and individuals	Tremendously voluminous and not quite available to all businesses or all people	Different types of discrimination against consumers
Consumers	Almost fully aware of their rather simple needs	Multiple-choice options and less aware of complex needs	Not catering to some consumer needs
Entrance of Enterprises	Very easy, no hindrances	In some industries it is almost impossible	Limited consumer alternatives
Pricing Dower	All are price takers	Most are price makers	Consumer discrimination
Promotion	Almost no need because Of closeness to the market	A major competitive advantage factor	Consumers are unduly influenced

Source: Adapted and revised from Samli (1992).

are relatively fewer firms (at least those that are in control), and many of them are very big. These extremely large firms can easily make an impact on the market and change the procedures of conducting business. The net impact of this total reversal has been a limitation of choice and a reduction in the negotiation power that consumers enjoyed.

In Adam Smith's market, business decision areas were very simple. Only a few basic decisions were made. It was simply taking care of present business. It involved no planning or strategic activity, no human resource management, no pricing or the like. It was almost natural for business to make simplistic, few and very basic decisions. In Clinton's current market, businesses have many complex problems dealing not only with the present but also the future. Businesses make multiple decisions simultaneously, and these decisions are extremely complex. The impact on the consumer is that in many cases businesses are preoccupied with their competitive positions and, hence, are making decisions to enhance their competitive advantage. These are somewhat removed from the consumer. Oftentimes, a business' preoccupation with competitors diverts it from customer needs and from their immediate markets.

In Adam Smith's market, information for businesses was very limited. In essence, businesses did not need much information. Furthermore each business (somewhat justifiably) was assumed to know what was needed to run a simple business. Information was also assumed to be totally available to consumers. Thus, books in economics talked about perfect knowledge on the part of businesses as well as consumers. In today's market, information is extremely voluminous, complex, costly to obtain and not readily available to all businesses and even less available to consumers. The lack of information on the part of the typical consumer leads to various types of discriminatory practices against consumers. If consumers don't have information, naturally they are bound to make bad decisions and are likely to be taken advantage of.

Consumers in Adam Smith's market were almost fully aware of their rather simple needs and all the choices to satisfy them. However, in the modern American market, consumers face multiple-choice options. Their needs are much more complex and their awareness of their own needs is not quite perfect. All consumers, are not satisfied. Many needs of many consumer groups, therefore, remain unanswered.

In the simpler world of Adam Smith, companies entered the market at free will and with great ease. Such flexibility gave consumers good choice and reasonable buys, since the competition was rather keen. In the modern market, however, competition is quite stifled with oligopolistic conditions. Once a few very powerful firms are controlling a large portion of the market, it is almost impossible to enter the market and compete with these giants. As a result, consumers have more limited alternatives than would be if there was more competition.

Since all companies were small and somewhat similar, pricing in Adam Smith's market was not a factor to vary and compete with. All firms were price takers in the sense that in an almost perfect competition, if the firm raised its price, it would lose all of its market. In Clinton's modern market, the firms are price makers. Particularly in oligopolistic situations, if the firm can differentiate itself, then it establishes the price it wants, and the lack of competition would allow such a pricing approach to be unchallenged. Certainly, the conditions, under oligopoly, are not favorable for the consumer. There is discrimination against the consumer.

Because of the simplicity of the market and the assumption of near-perfect knowledge, in the world of Adam Smith, promotion or advertising was simply not necessary. In Clinton's modern market, advertising, or promotion, plays a very critical role as a competitive advantage factor. Thus, a major portion of large oligopolistic firms' total efforts and resources goes to extensive promotion of the firm to differentiate it from its competitors. Such efforts unduly influence consumers and usually prevent them from making the best consumption or purchase decisions. The Internet is also disseminating pseudo information and questionable facts at an accelerated pace. This unchecked deluge of information further confuses consumers.

As the power in the modern market becomes more and more distorted, (particularly certain groups of consumers, see chapter 3) the equal opportunity prospects of consumers become less and less realistic.

THE TWO DEMOCRACIES

Samli (1992) posited that there are two democracies. While the first democracy is one person, one vote, the second democracy is one dollar, one vote. Perhaps the most important aspect of a democratic society is that if these two democracies check and balance each other, then they reinforce each other. This is the ideal situation. It indicates that consumers in that society can truly be equal opportunity consumers. Samli (1992) goes on to state that only through the balance of these two democracies can the equal opportunity consumer concept be converted from a myth to a reality.

Exhibit 4–2 illustrates different alternatives regarding the relationship between the two democracies. Because of the deteriorating distribution of income and accumulation of too much economic power in the hands of a few, at this point in time the American economy may be placed in the lower left quadrant of the diagram. Left alone, it is quite possible that it may move in the direction of the lower right quadrant. If the American society moves in that direction, the outcome will be disastrous for the American consumer as well as the nation's economy as a whole.

If, however, the American economy were to move in the direction of the upper left quadrant, then the American consumer will be truly empowered and the business sector as a whole will enjoy optimum profit levels. Such a goal cannot materialize automatically all by itself. The two democracies must be in balance so that brute economic power will not take over.

Exhibit 4–2
The Relationship Between the Two Democracies

	Good Political Democracy Poor	
Good **Economic** **Democracy**	Ideal situation. Good distribution of power and income.	Corrupting the goodness of the existing economic democracy when the economy is doing well.
     Poor	Uneven distribution of income. Increasing gap among economic classes.	Disaster for the American consumer as well as the American economy.

Exhibit 4–3 illustrates what could happen if the two democracies get further away from each other and both get weaker. This situation at least would lead in the direction of further deterioration of competition in the economy. Such a movement will further enhance the concentration of economic power in the hands of a few companies and of a fraction of the total population. This situation, by definition, will contribute to a widening gap between the haves and have nots, hence eliminating all chances of achieving an equal opportunity consumer society. Under these circumstances, while the quality of life for a privileged few is going up, for a very large majority of the population there will be a significant deterioration in quality of life, leading to serious political unrest and even class war.

Exhibit 4–3
The Negative Movement

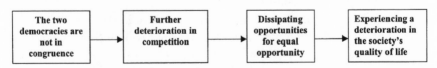

Source: Adapted and revised from Samli (1992).

Perhaps one of the most critical contributors to such an undesirable situation is the concentrated power of high tech. Since knowledge is power and in our society power is rewarded with wealth, modern technology plays a critical role in the formation of political democracy.

THE POWER OF HIGH TECH

When Naisbitt (1982) described one of the major changes, or in his terminology, one of the megatrends, by articulating the movement from an industrial society to an information society, he did not specify that the power of high tech would be so profound and so highly concentrated in the hands of a few companies and a small proportion of the total population. The information society is developing information technology (IT) which is, according to some researchers, replacing workers. According to some estimates, for every 1 percent increase in IT investment, average employment drops 0.13 percent (Aley 1994). Furthermore, technological illiteracy is widespread, and the few jobs generated by IT require high-level skills. These jobs pay extremely well and make a negative impact on the positive income distribution requirement for the empowerment of the American consumer.

THE SKILLS GAP

In addition to possibly decreasing the demand for more workers, IT requires high-level technological skills. However, more and more industries, ranging from high tech to aircraft to financial services, are not able to locate qualified people for employment. The lack of necessary basic technical skills is making the situation worse (Barron and Marsh 1998).

Since 1970, almost all income gains in the American economy have gone to the highest earning 20 percent of total households. This development created an income inequality that is unmatched in the world and in history since the Great Depression (Lardner 1998). In fact at this writing Bill Gates alone is wealthier than half the American people put together. Thus, high tech is leading to high power which, again, goes against empowering the American consumer.

Income inequality is exacerbated by the Federal Reserve Board's policies. When the Fed increases interest rates to cope with inflationary pressures, it creates additional unemployment. Increased unemployment enhances economic inequality. From the early 1970s through the mid-1980s and again in the early 1990s, the Federal Reserve's unstable and high interest rates produced high unemployment, and wage inequality went up. (Galbraith 1998). The highly skilled workers not only found better and higher paying jobs, but there was no disruption in their employment.

Thus, high tech and more sophisticated skills create high power. This is, in essence, the power of knowledge.

THE POWER OF KNOWLEDGE

While high-tech jobs tend to pay well, they also reflect the increasing complexity of society and the selectivity of this sector in creating jobs. As our society is moving in the direction of an information society rather than an industrial society (Naisbitt 1982; Drucker 1999) the power of knowledge is becoming clearer.

It is obvious that all countries, all industries and all businesses will, in their decisions, have to take into serious consideration their competitive standing in the world economy and the competitiveness of their knowledge competencies.

Although the fruits of knowledge, such as a piece of equipment or some special software, can be bought or sold, it is the knowledge that created the fruit that will take a long time to transfer (if at all). Such knowledge in the information society is concentrating in the hands of a few privileged groups or individuals. This is an alarming development that will cause much unrest in the marketplace.

Not only does the acquisition of knowledge have a cost, but it cannot be quite readily acquired by all. Hence, empowerment of the American consumer from this particular perspective is becoming less likely. Thinkers of our times maintain that a social transformation is necessary to remedy this situation. In order for a social transformation to take place, there must be a series of priorities regarding education.

- We must decide on the role of education, its purpose, its values and its content.
- The quality and productivity of knowledge must be established.
- The role of education must be identified in a country's competitiveness and, hence, it must be questioned how education policy must be changed so that the country's competitiveness can be enhanced.
- We must determine the responsibilities of knowledge. Particularly highly specialized knowledge must find its place in education (Drucker 1999).

The last point relates to extremely specialized knowledge that is used in the production of most modern systems. The Reagan years in the United States saw the highest military spending in peacetime. Extremely high military budgets were allocated to the development of highly sophisticated weapons systems that required special knowledge and skills. Those who possessed such knowledge and skills were a few privileged people who received extremely high salaries.

This situation, if contrasted with the preparation activity for World War II, explains why WWII was an antidepression measure, whereas the military preparedness during the Cold War era led into a major discrepancy in income distribution. It can easily be said that such an extreme discrepancy in the distribution of national income can easily cause economic recession and, what is more, if this situation is not quickly remedied, this recession can turn into a long-term poor performance on the part of the economy. This is because if only a few get very rich and the rest of society's income remains at the same level or gets further behind, then the aggregate demand of society shrinks. This shrinkage causes less than full employment and less than full utilization of society's productive facilities. Less than full utilization of productive facilities creates high costs as employment goes down. This is what happened during the stagflation of the late 1970s.

Of course, during the 1970s, 1980s and early 1990s, the economy did not grow much. Instead of investing in the nation's infrastructure (i.e., roads, warehouses, bridges, energy, communication and education) that would have facilitated economic growth, much was spent on national defense. The activity of producing military hardware is not quite as effective for economic development as investing in infrastructure. Thus, the misallocation of its resources did not help American society, and certainly it did not bring society to a point where more and more consumers improved their economic well-being.

CONTRASTING WAR PREPARATION IN THE 1940S AND THE 1980S

As was passingly referred to earlier, although in both war periods major national resources were allocated to military preparedness, the economic impact was considerably different. Prior to World War II, manufacturing and technology were considerably simpler than in the 1980s or today. Hence, manufacturing was substantially more labor—intensive. As a result, spending for military preparedness provided many jobs for many people. Thus, during that period, unemployment went down and incomes increased. But most of

Exhibit 4–4
National Defense and Education Spending in the United States

	National Defense	Education	Education as a Percent of Defense
1980	133,995	31,843	23.8
1985	252,748	29,342	11.6
1990	299,331	38,755	12.9
1995	272,066	54,263	19.9
1997 (Est.)	267,176	51,291	19.1

Source: U.S. Office of Management and Budget (1998).

all, distribution of income was such that special small groups did not get the "lion's share." The distribution was quite equitable. However, as technology became more and more sophisticated and weapon systems became more and more complex, the production process used to produce military weaponry became significantly more capital-intensive. The need for people, therefore, concentrated on a few, very highly skilled people.

Thus, military preparedness of the Cold War era created a few extremely rich millionaires, whereas military preparedness of early 1940s created many middle-class-income people. Hence, consumer empowerment, in reality, declined from the 1940s to the 1980s as income accumulated in fewer and fewer hands. Increasing complexity in military spending, therefore, created significant income inequity and negative empowerment of the American consumer. Thus, once again complexity created more complexity. The total military spending remained reasonably constant. In constant dollars, it was 4.9 percent of the gross domestic product (GDP) in 1980 and is estimated to be 3.4 percent of GDP in 1997, expressed in (1987) constant dollars (U.S. Office of Management and Budget 1998). However, spending on education, which already was substantially lower than military spending, did not increase at all. Exhibit 4–4 illustrates this point. In 1980, spending on education was about 23.8 percent of the total defense spending. In 1997, according to estimates, this percentage was about 19.1. It can be seen that the increasing complexity of society and, in this particular case, of weaponry, did not create a greater commitment to education.

First, education in itself has become more complex and more costly, which complicates the situation. But its not being shared with larger and larger groups of people in society has caused even more complications. This process is ongoing, and education in our society is abused by many *power* groups who are rather afraid of it. People in general are afraid of the unknown. Many less-educated people in power have been trying to keep our educational process under control by using divisive measures. Political, religious and some minorities are in this power-group classification.

These groups control our education system by promoting a big political appeal: *local authorities and parents rather than the federal government should decide on our children's education.* However, at no time has this stance brought about questions such as: How competent are the local authorities or parents? How do we determine that they are competent in making serious decisions as to the future of our children? Consider a community, for instance, where the majority of people are not even high school graduates. Now, assuming that such a community can make the best possible decisions regarding the education of its youth is truly a ludicrous proposition. What would a person with less than a high school diploma know about physics, chemistry, or algebra? The children of that community are bound to receive, at best, a mediocre education. The best education systems in the world are all highly centralized, not decentralized. Japan, Germany, France are all in that group. Currently, in the United States, Congress does not even allow a national competency testing for children, let alone allow a nationally standardized education. As the education system becomes more fragmented, the complexity of the problem is enhanced.

PRIVATIZATION OF EDUCATION

At the writing of this book, the Republican majority in the U.S. Congress has been pushing for privatization of our educational system. The first step in this direction is the *voucher system.* Giving vouchers to families to send their kids to private and religious schools will do nothing for the American education system. In fact, taking out a few of the better students from public schools and allowing them to go, say, to an unaccredited religious school is totally harmful for those children as well as the public education system. The whole process is based on tax credits. Therefore, in addition to questionable nature of the voucher system, this procedure forces the public to support certain religious doctrines in society. Additionally, while the public schools are neglected and need much attention, large proportions of public monies will go to private schools through these vouchers. This is not solving the U.S. public education problem. Rather, it creates much more complication. All citizens are entitled to education. But privatization of education makes it a privilege for a select few.

SUMMARY

This chapter reiterates the fact that our society is very complex, and simplistic solutions or unchecked complexity begets more and more complexity. The chapter first presents a contrast between Adam Smith's market and the present American market. The modern American market is much more complex and much less prone to empowering the American consumer. It is much less competitive. A discussion of democracy explores the fairness of the system. There are two democracies: political democracy is one person, one vote. Economic democracy is one dollar, one vote. The chapter claims that these two democracies are not congruent. This situation would lead to further deterioration of competition and society by allowing economic power to accumulate in the hands of a few. This complicates the situation further.

Technological advances are a major factor in the deterioration of income distribution. There are fewer and fewer who have the technological training to make very large sums. The production of modern weapon systems also complicates the situation further by enhancing the present economic inequality. Finally, the education system, under the influence of certain power groups, is delivering less and less. Hence, as the complexity of society increases, empowerment possibilities deteriorate.

REFERENCES

Aley, James (1994). "High Tech Vs Jobs," *Fortune*, April 4, 30–31.

Barron, Kelly, and Marsh, Ann (1998). "The Skills Gap: Why Do We Have a Worker Shortage in a Society with Considerable Residual Unemployment?" *Forbes*, February 23, 44–46.

Champion, Sandra (1988). "Technostress: Technology Toll," *School Library Journal*, November, 48–51.

Drucker, Peter F. (1999). *Management Challenges for the 21st Century*. New York: HarperBusiness.

Galbraith, James K. (1998). "The Fed's Modest Agenda," *The New York Times*, August 28, A23.

Lardner, James (1998). "A New Health Hazard: Economic Inequality," *The Washington Post National Weekly Edition*, August 24, 44.

McConnell, Sheila (1996). "The Role of Computers in Reshaping the Work Force," *Monthly Labor Review*, August, 3–5.

Naisbit, John (1982). *Megatrends*. New York: Warnerbooks.

Samli, A. Coskun (1992). *Social Responsibility in Marketing*. Westport, CT: Quorum Books.

U.S. Office of Management and Budget (1998). *Historical Tables*. Washington, DC: U.S. Government Printing Office.

The Magnificent American Economy

There is no other country in the world nor has there ever been a country where about 4 percent of the population feeds all 100 percent. The American agricultural sector can easily do this, and it has so much extra food remaining that it is used to help countries where there may be serious food shortage problems.

The American economy is the largest in the world. It has the highest standards of living in terms of automobile ownership, radio ownership, computer ownership and so forth. It has the highest productivity along with the highest industrial capacity. The way it performs, however, is not at optimum potential. The American economy can grow faster in real terms and can almost eradicate poverty within the country, but, again, without proper empowerment of the American consumer, these most important goals cannot materialize.

SIZE LEADS TO ECONOMIES OF SCALE

The concept of economies of scale is perhaps the force behind the industrialization of advanced societies of the world. If the productive facilities of the country are used properly—that is, in the way they should be—and fully, the cost of production goes down. Thus, producing large quantities reduces

Exhibit 5–1
Index of Manufacturing Capacity

YEAR	INDEX OF CAPACITY	RELATIONSHIP OF OUTPUT TO CAPACITY
1990	121	81
1991	123	78
1992	126	80
1993	128	81
1994	134	83
1995	136	83
1996	142	82

1992 output = 100

Source: Statistical Abstract of the United States 1997 (Washington, DC: U.S. Department of Commerce), 750.

cost and utilizes economies of scale. However, if society wants to benefit from the use of economies of scale, then there must be an adequate aggregate demand in that society to support such utilization. In other words, an economy of mass production, which is essential to maintain the industrial fabric of society, cannot exist without mass consumption. If there is no adequate demand, the production sector will function at less than full capacity levels. Hence, once again, consumer empowerment becomes the focal point. If there is not an equitable distribution of income and if consumers do not have sufficient confidence that they will still have a job tomorrow, next month, next year, then they will not buy these products and be an actual part of the aggregate demand. It must be realized that the magnificent productive capacity that exists will not be used adequately if the aggregate demand is adequate and/or people don't want to spend their money because they are not feeling secure.

Exhibit 5–1 illustrates the utilization of the industrial capacity in the United States. As can be seen, between 1990 and 1996, there have been very minor variations in capacity utilization. About 20 percent of the U.S. industrial capacity is still not used. At the point of writing this book, this author thinks that this is a very high proportion of the total productive capacity (about one-fifth).

It is possible, perhaps, to absorb another 10 percent of that productive capacity along with about 1 percent of the 4.5 percent of the existing unemployment. This, by definition, broadens the economic base of the country and enables more people to be independent and empowered through well-paying jobs in the industrial sector of the economy.

But how do we manage to connect the unemployed with the unused industrial capacity? In the past, ambitious large firms may have attempted to accomplish bringing unemployment and unused capacity together by expansion and by attempting to capture a large share of the market. However, as discussed in earlier chapters, in recent years American firms have been opting for the short-run bottom line by downsizing and scaling down operations. Merger mania that was discussed in earlier chapters does not expand operations physically. In almost all cases of mergers, there is downsizing, which does not result in absorbing unused capacity.

Thus, unless small firms make an attempt to absorb the unemployed, there will not be much progress. But small businesses almost always function at the margin, just one step away from failure. They do not have extra resources or access to extra funds to expand their businesses. Finally, if there are excess capacities, they are not likely to be in small business. It is therefore quite clear that the American economy is not benefiting from economies of scale. Thus, American consumers are not getting much of the fruits of the modern economy. The magnificent American economy needs support from the enterprises to absorb its capacity totally and to use its human resources fully, so that economies of scale will materialize and benefit the whole society.

WHAT ABOUT ECONOMIES OF SCOPE AND SPEED?

As seen in the previous section, economies of scale are not materializing. Thus, those who are justifying merger mania as the "enhancement of the opportunity to capitalize on economies of scales" are not correct. There is no evidence to indicate that merger mania is moving in the direction of reducing the unused industrial capacity of the United States. In recent years, two other terms have entered the literature: economies of scope and economies of speed.

Economies of scope imply that a large firm can produce multiple outputs. In such cases, all outputs can be produced at a lesser cost of producing the same level of outputs in separate production activity (Gonzales 1997). Many multiproduct, multiservice companies thus have the advantage of scope through their large size and coordination. But such economies of scope may go against economies of scale. Companies may be scaling down their mass production capabilities while enhancing their scope economies. These companies are competing somewhat unfairly if the economies of scale they forego are greater than the economies of scope they gain. Moreover, this is accomplished by creating very large organizations through merger mania.

Once again, because of their very large size, these companies are not responsive to consumer needs, not very close to markets and not very flexible. They can do certain things very well, but they cannot deviate. They cannot quickly respond to newly emerging market opportunities. If a large company creates a void in terms of competition by buying out major competitors and then provides a series of limited products and services and generates economies of scope, these products and services will sell better with the company's name. Just what is the net result to the economy in the marketplace? There is, unfortunately, little evidence in either way. Certainly, if the company is doing its utmost to capitalize on economies of scale and scope, these two can be additive and synergistic. Such synergism would be very beneficial to the whole society, including, of course, all consumers.

Finally *economies of speed* indicate that such a large company can more successfully bring about some products or services to the market. However, whether or not it truly takes advantage of economies of speed is another question. Certainly, when VW developed the new Beetle or Microsoft introduced Windows 98, these companies took advantage of economies of speed; however, much of the time economies of speed reinforce and enhance the economic power that these companies command. If enhancing such competitive advantage, by way of scales or speed, does not benefit the consumer in general, but provides much economic power for the company by its sheer size and financial power, then it is questionable if such economic power benefits the consumer.

The magnificence of the American economy is such that it allows and indeed encourages these three economies: scale, scope and speed. It is maintained here that if all three take place simultaneously, there will be a synergistic impact. However, without economies of scale, there will be no social benefit toward empowerment of the consumer through economies of scope and speed. They are likely to benefit the company at the expense of consumers. These propositions are not carefully researched as yet, but it is proposed here that any activity, event or procedure that enhances the economic power of extra-large firms, without outreach to benefit more and more consumers through employment, product quality, savings through price and environmental benefits, provides no net gain toward the empowerment of the American consumer. While these three scales, particularly if they do not coexist, may not make a contribution when the industrial giants are considered, they certainly make a positive impact when entrepreneurial activity is concerned. The three scales can easily be accomplished by smaller lean, mean competing machines. In other words, small entrepreneurial enterprises can accomplish such a coexistence among the economies of scale, scope and speed. Such synergistic accomplishments would certainly improve the economy and enhance the consumer empowerment.

ENTREPRENEURIAL SPIRIT AND PERFORMANCE

Perhaps one of the most impressive aspects of the magnificent American economy is the existence of entrepreneurial opportunities. Every year thousands of new firms enter the market along with thousands of new products. Sometimes one of these newly emerging businesses becomes a huge success. The American economy not only allows such events to take place but actually encourages supersuccessful entrepreneurs to become very successful. Consider, for instance, the following:

- A young employee of Hewlett-Packard in 1976 tried to convince his managers that personal computers were marketable items. Subsequently he cofounded *Apple Computers, Inc.*
- The young man's father told him that he was not smart enough to be an employee in his retail store. Just to show him, the young man started his retail store that was the beginning of *The Limited.*
- Two brothers in Detroit had an Italian restaurant that was failing. One brother decided that he would work on the auto assembly line. The other brother decided to concentrate on pizzas and home delivery. This was the beginning of *Domino's Pizza.*

Developing a new business or expanding an existing one depends on the effective use of technology, physical resources, human resources and money. But above all, such a development requires a catalyst or an agent that is called the entrepreneur (Samli and Gimple 1985). A business cannot start all by itself, even though there are great windows of opportunity, adequate technical skills and sufficient capital, among other necessities, to start a business. All of these resources must be brought together, matched against the established opportunity range and directed properly so that the new venture will be a success. It is the entrepreneur who performs these duties and makes a reality out of just an idea.

Entrepreneurs are critical agents of change in the American economy. They could promote the drive for the increasingly efficient use of resources and stimulate trade among various parties or factions in society with different preferences, skills and endowments. They are critical in the areas of self-employment, new job creation (Arzeni 1997) and innovation of new ideas, concepts and products. It has been stated that in all these areas they do better than very large industrial giants.

A CONTRAST BETWEEN ENTREPRENEURSHIP AND LARGE CORPORATIONS

Up to this point, it is posited that one of the most important features of the spectacular American economy is its support for entrepreneurship. It is implied here that small businesses are all entrepreneurships. All small businesses may not be quite entrepreneurial in the sense that true entrepreneurship is likely to have some type of a new idea or innovation along with its status of being a small business. However, most small businesses need to be quite entrepreneurial if they are to survive. Without a new idea, a new service or a new product line, a small new business is not entrepreneurial enough and cannot survive competition. Exhibit 5–2 illustrates how entrepreneurships differ from large corporations and, therefore, why they are more consumer-oriented and help enhance consumer empowerment in our society. The exhibit identifies five key points: proximity, flexibility, ability, creativity and affinity.

Proximity is related to the entrepreneur's closeness to consumers and the market. As consumer needs change and market conditions vary, entrepreneurs can detect these developments very early because of their proximity. Large corporations, on the other hand, are becoming less and less accessible by consumers because they are becoming further and further removed from consumers and the market. When NationsBank merged with Barnett Bank, they closed down a number of customer centers and local banking facilities. Hence, they became less accessible.

Flexibility refers to ability in making decisions. Entrepreneurships are not bogged down by bureaucracies, red tape, rules and strategic plans. As market conditions change, they can make quick, easy and creative adjustments. In large corporate entities, the decision-making process is typically belabored by checks and balances which are activated by internal controls, bureaucratic layers, red tape and other organizational barriers to speedy decision-making.

Exhibit 5–2
A Contrast Between Entrepreneurship and Large Corporations

	Entrepreneurship	Large Corporation
Proximity	Closer to the consumer and the market	Removed from the consumer and the market
Flexibility	Can make decisions and move speedily	The decision-making process is belabored by checks and balances
Problem-Solving Ability	Real understanding of problems accelerates development of resolutions	Far removed from problems; cannot generate fast, practical and different solutions
Creativity	Is not bogged down with conventional wisdom	Conventional wisdom and past experiences interfere with clear thinking
Affinity problems	Identification with the market and consumer problems	Lack of ability to comprehend market needs and consumer problems

Ability here means problem-solving ability. Real understanding of the consumer and market problems accelerates the development of real practical and effective solutions. Since large corporations are far removed from consumer or market problems, they have difficulty comprehending the problem, let alone generating fast and practical solutions.

Perhaps the most important feat we can say of entrepreneurs is that they are creative and are not bogged down with conventional wisdom. They find new, practical and marketable solutions to emerging consumer problems. Conventional wisdom, among others, is like saying "we tried that and it does not work." But it might, under different circumstances. Large corporations typically do not encourage or exercise creativity. Their conventional wisdom interferes with the clear thinking that leads to creativity. They are much concerned with propagating the "corporate culture" and generating "organization men."

Affinity here refers to being very close to the market and consumers and, hence, thinking like them and therefore having a real feeling about consumer problems. Larger corporations lack this particular ability. They cannot quickly and adequately comprehend consumer problems.

It is rather clear from this discussion that entrepreneurial ventures are very good for solving consumer problems satisfactorily and enhancing consumer empowerment. Entrepreneurial ventures also generate much-needed jobs at grassroots levels (Finley 1990). Finally, entrepreneurial ventures enhance competition at the consumer level, the outcome of which is critically in the best interest of the typical American consumer. The role entrepreneurs play in competition is particularly critical, since early on in this book we discussed how competition in American markets is on the decline.

COMPETITION DOES NOT BEAT COMPETITION

Competition does not beat competition, but merger mania does. It is the biggest way to beat competition. In earlier years of the twentieth century, American industry behaved rather differently in the marketplace. For instance, mergers and acquisitions were primarily related to those companies that were at the brink of failure. They were bought out by others who planned to improve the conditions and attempted to make them profitable. However, in the later part of the same century things have completely changed. Companies as part of the merger mania bought out competitors that happened to be very entrepreneurial and doing well. Some of the time after the merger, some parts of the company are sold out or closed down and, hence, the competition is partly eliminated, the profitability is somewhat enhanced and the market share is improved. Thus, although entrepreneurship at the beginning poses competition to already existing large firms, if some of these new and dynamic entrants excel in the marketplace and start becoming a threat or at least quite a profitable venture, then one of the larger firms attempts to buy them out. As a result, competition in the marketplace declines, and some firms become larger and larger, not because they are good and serving the market well but because they have large financial resources.

As these companies become larger and the market becomes more oligopolistic, entry into the market becomes more and more difficult. As competition subsequently ends up begetting less competition, two major threats take away the benefits that entrepreneurial ventures naturally offer to the society: first, dynamic and competitive firms that are performing well are bought out and somewhat pacified by large firms that are not clearly as beneficial to consumers; and second, as the large firms become larger through such acquisitions, it becomes more difficult for new entrepreneurial companies to enter the marketplace.

However, the threat to entrepreneurship is not only from large and pow-erful firms, but also from market conditions and the lack of available support. Market conditions may become extremely adverse and, as a result, small entrepreneurial firms are most likely the first ones to get hurt (Samli 1993). In 1995, for instance, over 71,000 businesses failed. Of these, over 51,000 went bankrupt. These are very large numbers if we consider, for instance, the 1981 figures that were 17,000 and 47,000 failures and bankruptcies, re-spectively (Statistical Abstract of the United States 1997). The cost to society in such cases is very large, and the harm done to consumers because of failures and bankruptcies is very far-reaching.

It would take special programs and special effort to minimize failures among entrepreneurial ventures in recessionary periods. Unfortunately, such programs do not exist, with perhaps the one exception of the incubator concept that is made available in some inner cities of large metropolitan areas. These incubators provide a protective atmosphere for newly organized small businesses. They also provide consulting, funds and other types of support. However, much of the time major support is given to larger firms because of their economic and related political power. These large firms can negotiate with communities to get extraordinary tax and location advantages. Furthermore, they threaten the community by saying that if there are no additional favors, the company will relocate elsewhere and eliminate thou-sands of local jobs. Thus, entrepreneurial ventures, however valuable, are not in business for prolonged periods of time. This hurts consumers' chances to be further empowered.

It must be emphasized here that large corporations can also act entrepre-neurial. Although not so common, the term *intrapreneurship* refers to this situation. Implementation of a culture of intrapreneurship within companies refers to encouraging innovative activity by implementing an entrepreneurial climate in a corporate entity. Large companies with an entrepreneurial ap-proach encourage individuals who introduce, say, a new idea for a product or service to follow through to test its validity, to modify it further and try again. If the idea has merit, both the individual and the company benefit (Pryor and Shays 1993).

It has been stated that IBM, Motorola, 3M and other major American corporations have been experimenting with this concept. The idea revolves around trying to tap into the creative power of corporate members. Man-agers must recognize newly developing strategies, assess corporate readiness for these and reinforce the creative behavior with effective rewards (Kuratko et al. 1993). Such efforts indicate some degree of understanding and appreciation of entrepreneurial values. If large American companies were to develop such intrapreneurship values, then, most probably, the differences displayed in Exhibit 5–2 will disappear and movement toward closeness to consumer empowerment will be reinstated. But such an orientation is rather a management attitude and cannot be regulated or implemented by the government or a power group.

Understanding the fact that competition in the American economy has been deteriorating, since around mid-1970s or so, an outside effort has been made to stimulate competition. To this effect, deregulation has been advocated and implemented by both political parties.

DEREGULATION AND COMPETITION

Although it was meant to enhance competition, the deregulation movement that started during the 1970s did not quite prove to be performing what it was originally intended to perform. More on this topic is presented in chapter 7. However, suffice it to say that deregulation is not helping the magnificent American economy to capitalize on its potential. This is partly because the proponents of deregulation believe in *all* or *nothing at all*. They think deregulation should be total, all regulation is bad and all deregulation is good. Their understanding of "free" market is free of government regulation. But the world is not black or white and there are not always two alternatives, either pro or con. Rigid thinking is more apt to hurt the economy than help.

Some industries may need to be deregulated; however, there are others that need perhaps to be regulated so that competition can be enhanced. In other words, regulations could be for or against competition. The society would do well to regulate to enhance competition if, through deregulating, competition is hindered. For instance, the Sherman Antitrust Act prohibits monopolies and attempts to monopolize; the Clayton Act prohibits specified monopolistic practices; and the Celler-Kefauver Act prohibits asset acquisition which tends toward monopoly. Any one of these, if not enforced or banned, will enhance the chance to create monopolies; therefore, deregulation in such cases is most likely to be harmful. On the other hand, the Miller-Tydings Act or the McGuire-Keogh Act legalized practices that reduced competition (Anderson, Bentley and Sharpe 1976).

Thus, indiscriminant deregulation will not enhance competition. It will create anarchy in the American market. Selective deregulation and certainly selective regulation must always be considered for maintaining competition in our society that has served us so well. If competition is not maintained, not the fit but the fat is likely to survive because it can buy out the lean and mean competitors, and its motives will never be questioned. This certainly can go on indefinitely, or until the value of competition is recognized and attempts to oligopolize or monopolize are disrupted.

One of the most important points that needs to be remembered here is that the market does not really have a consciousness, and it cannot plan all by itself to maintain competition. The market only reacts. Much of the time such a reaction will be at the last moment after a major event such as the stock market crash in 1929 that led the American society into the Great Depression. Only planned precautionary measures could remedy the part that the market cannot accomplish. The market would only react to lack of competition. It cannot therefore plan to prevent such a trend. This is where regulation to enhance competition becomes very critical. In order to prevent the market from reacting uncontrollably and sharply, it may be necessary to clarify what types of regulations in which industries will enable optimal economic activity and balanced growth so that the consumer will be empowered.

CREATION OF A BALANCED GROWTH: A HYPOTHETICAL ANALYSIS

The top portion of Exhibit 5–3 illustrates the relative income of the top fifth, 2nd fifth, 3rd fifth, 4th fifth, and the bottom fifth of the population in different years. First of all, it can be seen that the gap between the incomes of the lowest fifth of the population and the highest fifth has been growing in an accelerated manner. While in 1970 the top fifth made almost $20,000 more than the lowest fifth, in 1995 this difference was more than $100,000. An assumption is made and a question is raised: What if the lowest fifth of the American society were to receive the median income of the total?

In 1995, the median income was $45,338.6, and the new median income was $52,736.3. In other words, the median income had increased by 16.3 percent. By taking this increase of 16.3 percent in the income of the lowest fifth of the population, an analysis was performed on the unused industrial production capacity, how many new jobs would the increased utilization of the industrial capacity, what would be the new level of industrial shipments and, based on this new level of shipments, how many more new employees are added. Exhibit 5–4 illustrates these calculations. As can be seen, some 31 million workers are added, and the new level of capacity utilization goes up to almost 97 percent. These analyses indicate that the magnificent American economy is capitalizing less than the optimal capacity because of the very low earning levels of the lowest fifth of the population. It is obvious

Exhibit 5-3
Creation of Balanced Growth, 1970–95

Current dollars: Mean income received by each fifth (households as of March of the following year)

	1970	1975	1980	1985	1990	1995
Lowest fifth	2,029	3,034	4,483	5,797	7,195	8,350
Second fifth	5,395	7,204	10,819	14,333	18,030	20,397
Third fifth	8,688	11,787	17,807	23,735	29,781	34,106
Fourth fifth	12,247	17,117	26,219	35,694	44,901	54,429
Highest fifth	21,684	29,809	46,053	65,481	87,137	109,411
Total	**50,043**	**68,951**	**105,381**	**145,040**	**187,044**	**226,693**
Number of households	64,385	72,867	82,368	88,458	94,312	99,683
Median Income of total	**10,008.6**	**13,790.2**	**21,076.2**	**29,008**	**37,408.8**	**45,338.6**

If the Lowest fifth had the mean income of all categories

	1970	1975	1980	1985	1990	1995
Lowest fifth	10,008.6	13,790.2	21,076.2	29,008	37,408.8	45,338.6
Second fifth	5,395	7,204	10,819	14,333	18,030	20,397
Third fifth	8,688	11,787	17,807	23,735	29,781	34,106
Fourth fifth	12,247	17,117	26,219	35,694	44,901	54,429
Highest fifth	21,684	29,809	46,053	65,481	87,137	109,411
Total	**58,022.6**	**79,707.2**	**121,974.2**	**168,251**	**217,257.8**	**263,681.6**
Median Income of total	**11,604.52**	**15,941.44**	**24,394.84**	**33,650.2**	**43,451.56**	**52,736.32**

Bureau of Census, March 1999 population survey

	1970	1975	1980	1985	1990	1995
Median Income 1	10,008.6	13,790.2	21,076.2	29,008	37,408.8	45,338.6
Median Income 2	11,604.52	15,941.44	24,394.84	33,650.2	43,451.56	52,736.32
	1,595.92	2,151.24	3,318.64	4,642.2	6,042.76	7,397.72
Percentage variation	15.9454869	15.5997738	15.7459125	16.0031715	16.1533115	16.3166044

Source: *Statistical Abstract of the United States*, various issues.

Exhibit 5-4
Industrial Production & Capacity Utilization, 1995

Industry	Capacity utilization rates by major industry group	Value of shipments (mil $)	All employees (thousands)	Estimated value of shipments with 16.3% increase	Estimated number of employees corresponding to the 16.3% increase of the value of ship.	New capacity of utilization due to the 16.3% increase in percentage	Number of employees added due to this increase
All manufacturing establ	83.2	3,589,157	18,740	4,174,189	21,795	96.7615	
Food & Kindred products	81.5	448,405	1,526	521,495	1,849	94.7845	323
Tobacco products		32,984	31	38,360		0	
Textile mill products	83.6	79,742	607	92,739	717	97.22581	110
Apparel and other text pro	77.5	78,097	950	90,826	1,211	90.1317	261
Lumber & Wood products	84.7	104,923	741	122,025	864	98.50574	123
Furnitures & Fixtures	81.3	53,571	514	62,303	624	94.55179	110
Paper & Allied products	89.0	172,638	630	200,777	699	103.5065	69
Printing and Publishing	81.4	188,439	1,534	219,154	1,861	94.66796	327
Chemical & Allied Products	78.9	362,126	839	421,152	1,050	91.76058	211
Petroleum and coal pro	91.7	151,261	110	175,916	118	106.6468	8
Rubber & Misc. Plastic pro	91.0	145,426	1,018	169,130	1,105	105.8327	87
Leather & Leather pro	73.0	9,064	86	10,541	116	84.89552	30
Stone, clay & glass product	79.3	75,990	503	88,376	626	92.22551	123
Primary metal industries	91.1	180,303	688	209,692	746	105.9491	58
Fabricated metal products	84.3	204,819	1,465	238,204	1,716	98.0407	251
Industrial machinery & equip	90.2	351,114	1,926	408,345	2,109	104.9025	183
Electronics; other elec equip	87.3	299,837	1,534	348,710	1,736	101.5298	202
Transportation equipt	69.4	462,616	1,523	538,022	2,168	80.71214	645
Instruments & related products	77.6	140,910	809	163,878	1,030	90.24862	221
Misc manuf industries	77.6	46,891	397	54534	505	90.24841	108

Source: Statistical Abstract of the United States, various issues.

that if this sector made as much money as average Americans do, the whole society would be better off, and it must be emphatically reiterated that the total market will yield more profit for all. Perhaps a major consideration here is to raise minimum wages to a much higher level, as special incentives also are given to businesses not to reduce their number of employees. Again, as seen in Exhibits 5–3 and 5–4, what America as a whole is losing is much more than the increased hypothetical incomes of the lowest fifth of the population.

It is critical that this magnificent American economy follow a route of optimal growth with full employment, no excess capacities and maximum benefits to most American consumers. Such a growth pattern, I believe, is possible only if competition is maintained and merger mania is stopped. However, this is not quite enough, even though it is a necessary prerequisite. The economy must be diversified and those sectors that are the most promising receive (if necessary) government support in terms of infrastructure and stimulation. Part of the magnificence of the American market is its versatility. It does not have to emphasize only one industry and does not have to limit its explorations for new industries to develop. If the economy is allowed to grow in a diversified manner while maintaining a high level of competition, it is quite likely that all Americans (not only a few) will benefit.

SUMMARY

This chapter deals with the magnificence of the American economy. It points out that the American economy is not living up to its potential. One reason is the merger mania that is at least partially limiting the full utilization of resources. Furthermore, inadequate support for entrepreneurial and intrapreneurial behaviors is limiting or reducing the necessary levels of competition. Finally, deregulation is also seen as a factor limiting competition. The chapter ends with an argument for a balanced economic growth possibility. Here it is posited that given proper leadership and eliminating the attempts that are limiting competition, the American economy can move further and faster in the direction of using economies of scale, scope and speed by its mean, lean competing machines that would benefit all.

REFERENCES

Anderson, W. Thomas; Bentley, Catherine C.; and Sharpe, Louis K. (1976). *Multidimensional Marketing*. Austin, TX: Austin Press.

Arzeni, Sergio (1997). "Entrepreneurship and Job Creation," *OECO Observer*, December, 18–20.

Finley, Laurence (1990). *Entrepreneurial Strategies*. Boston: PWS-Kent Publishing Company.

Gonzales, Theresa L. (1997). "An Empirical Study of Economies of Scope in Home Healthcare," *Health Services Research*, August, 32, 313–325.

Kuratko, Donald F.; Hornsby, Jeffrey S.; Naffziger, Douglas W.; and Montagno, Ray V. (1993). "Implement Entrepreneurial Thinking in Established Organizations," *Advanced Management Journal*, Winter, 28–35.

Pryor, Austin K. and Shays, E. Michael (1993). "Growing the Business with Intrapreneurs." *Business Quarterly*, Spring, 42–50.

Samli, A. C. and Gimple, Martin L. (1985). "Transferring Technology to Generate Effective Entrepreneurs in Less Developed Countries," in A. C. Samli (ed.), *Technology Transfer*. Westport, CT: Quorum Books.

Samli, A. Coskun (1993). *Counterturbulence Marketing*. Westport, CT: Quorum Books.

Statistical Abstract of the United States 1997. Washington, DC: U.S. Department of Commerce.

Chapter 6

Federalism Versus States' Rights

In recent years, there has been an attack on the national government with an unprecedented passion and ferocity. Particularly the Republican party has apparently determined to destroy national standards, national projects and national regulations and transfer the governing authority from the national government to the states (Schlesinger 1995). But can these states truly run these programs better while they have less money and less experience (if any) than the federal government? In reality, most states do not really have programs in place. Many states may not be prepared for new responsibilities relating to issues such as welfare, job training, transportation and health. Furthermore, many local bodies can be as bureaucratic and ineffective as the feds and often far more corrupt (Kelly and Melcher 1995). Even if the states were equally competent and had the funds and willingness, it is maintained here that each state going in its own way independently to solve its problems, cannot possibly allow the American economy to optimize. As these states try to solve their problems independently and in an uncoordinated manner, America is likely to experience suboptimization in its overall endeavors.

OPTIMIZATION OF AN ECONOMY

Empowerment of the American consumer can take place particularly well if the economy is functioning at the optimal level. The optimization of

American economy can be described as follows: Imagine a classical orchestra of fifty of the best musicians in the world (one musician per state). Also, imagine fifty just average musicians. The first group does not have a conductor. The second group has a world-renowned conductor, say Zubin Mehta (a very-well-known conductor). Both orchestras are asked to play Beethoven's Fifth. Which group could make better music? Despite its extensive talent supply, the first orchestra cannot play very well since it has no leadership and hence no coordination. Each player will perform according to his or her ability without considering the relative role that he or she plays in the whole symphony. The second group more than makes up for the lacking deficiency in talent by being led by one of the best conductors in the world. No doubt, the second group is more likely to produce better music. It is easy to draw a parallel between this example and the American economy. Without proper leadership, the economy cannot optimize its activities and perform as well as it could and, hence, it cannot deliver the best conditions to the American consumer.

Adam Smith (1996 edition), in *Inquiry into the Nature and Causes of the Wealth of Nations*, posited that nations create value and wealth in the best possible way if they use division of labor. Each worker becomes a specialist and therefore more productive in performing a certain task. Thus, no one person (no state) could make everything he or she needs. A high level of productivity would yield enough value for an individual to exchange some of it for other things that this particular individual needs or desires. Earlier in this book, it is advocated that such a market, where each individual state is expected to be more of a specialist than simply a self-satisfying generalist, cannot be left alone totally unchecked. If unchecked, there will be a tendency to become generalists rather than specialists. However, the basic principle here is applicable to the American economy. If the American states were producing everything themselves for themselves, there would be much duplication and little (if any) specialization. Thus, there would be no opportunity to optimize the performance of the American economy and hence to improve consumer empowerment.

Assume, for instance, all fifty states try to be totally self-sufficient. Each will have an auto industry, a food industry, a pharmaceutical industry and so on. Assume that the states of California and Nevada are both trying to be self-sufficient in producing food. Therein lies the problem. Nevada cannot possibly be as productive in agriculture as California because of the climate, soil and even perhaps its people's attitude toward agriculture. Nevada is likely to be better off by perhaps emphasizing other things that California will not do and exchange goods and services with its neighboring state and pay credence to Adam Smith's division of labor concept. Together California and Nevada could achieve synergism. By each state concentrating on what it can do best and trading with others for additional needs, the principle of comparative advantage is achieved. If each state can concentrate on what it can best produce or perform, all states working together can create synergism.

Creating synergism can be related to developing local economic multipliers that would indicate the impact of certain investments in local economies. These multipliers are based on national input-output matrices. In other words, scientific measures such as input-output matrices can be used to determine which industries can yield the best economic results in terms of creating more and better jobs as well as expanding the economic base.

State governments are to be helped to determine the total impact of their policies. This determination can be based on economic multipliers that are calculated from national input-output matrices. In other words, if the total national economy and its changes are analyzed by determining what each state can do best and encouraged to do just that, the growth in the national economy will be optimized. This way each state can concentrate on the economically most beneficial activities that would create the greatest multipliers for investment rather than thinking of producing of their essential needs. Emphasizing the industries with the greatest multipliers creates *ripple effects* that are very desirable in economic base development (Hefner 1997).

DIVIDED THERE IS NO SYNERGISM

In essence, the United States is like a strong regional trade bloc. If this trade bloc is an ideal one, it would display a most diverse range of comparative advantage generation in that each partner would be performing in the areas in which it has special strengths. Hence, the bloc is creating a maximum amount of trade internally as well as externally (Kotler, Jatusripitak and Maesincee 1997).

Indeed, NAFTA and the European Union (EU) are economic arrangements in search of synergism, where individual parties bring something significant to the trade bloc. But the total economic wealth generation of the bloc as a whole is greater than what each member brings into the bloc, which is what synergism is all about. One of the most important features of the American economy also is that fifty partners are brought together in search of optimization and synergism. Together the fifty states under the direction of an effective government can generate more than what the sum of economic activity these individual states can generate if they were left alone on their own discretion regarding their economic activity. Thus, there is a major issue here that is being debated: federalism versus statism (or states' rights).

THE AMERICAN ECONOMY MUST NOT BE DIVIDED

If the American economy were to function as just the sum total of fifty independent components, in addition to the disappearing synergism and increasing duplication, there will be fifty bureaucracies instead of one. This is not a desirable but rather a dangerous state of affairs.

Beyond the level of normal administration, fifty bureaucracies can be extremely complex and counterproductive. It is quite inaccurate to claim that state governments are closer to the people and therefore they are more responsive to people's needs and concerns (Schlesinger 1995). Historically, the federal government has served better as the protector of the powerless workers, farmers, minorities, children, disabled and elderly (Schlesinger 1995). Without a strong federal government, these groups of consumers will not have much chance to become empowered to improve the economic quality of their lives. It is quite reasonable to posit that without the powers of the federal government, the desegregation of universities in the South would not have materialized! After all it was the states that created the prevailing segregation and without the federal government there would have been no incentive to reverse existing segregation.

It is maintained that nationally administered Social Security and Medicare are much better run than state-administered welfare and Medicaid. Similarly, for example, it is easier to conduct antituberculosis programs nationally than to allow each state to run its own program. This has been the case since the 1970s, and nationally the problem of tuberculosis has gotten much worse (Schlesinger 1995). Indeed many programs that are critical for consumers' well-being will be discontinued because many states do not have the vision, inclination or even the resources to pursue improvement in those areas such as antidiscrimination activity. With states' rightist orientation to school desegregation, in some of the southern states, school desegregation programs may not have taken place at all. Thus, the lack of continuity in states rightist orientation will create a very checkered posture in the nation for the American consumer. This is almost saying some consumers will have to choose where they get education, medical care, equal opportunity for jobs and a fair treatment as consumers.

Two particular areas must be specifically examined, *scientific research* and *infrastructure development*. First, scientific research, particularly basic research that does not show immediate returns in terms of generating income, is not likely to be undertaken by the states in a meaningful manner. Indeed it has been stated that if states' rights were to go in the direction as it is desired by some politicians, that movement will threaten the very foundations of science in this country (Schlesinger 1995). Second, infrastructure development will not be treated properly. If left to individual states, there will be no coordination in this extremely important activity. It is, for instance, easy to see the problem that could occur when one state's six-lane highway connects in the next state to a two-lane highway. Suddenly the heavy traffic from the first state comes to a halt in the second state because of traffic bottlenecks. In other words, infrastructure development would become a nationwide patchwork of state-based infrastructure development activity. Such a development cannot possibly create infrastructural synergism.

Of course, the same things can be said about almost all of the major issues that profoundly influence consumers' quality of life. Among these major issues are welfare, transportation, Medicaid, job-training and environment. All of these critical areas, if left up to individual states, would create a patchwork of state-based regulations. The lack of continuity coupled with the lack of economic synergism will create a very difficult situation, particularly for certain groups of consumers who do not have a lot of resources to get ahead or to sustain certain levels of economic, social, educational and health-related lifestyles. They may have to pick and choose where they will live if they have the means to move around. But those who are immobile and devoid of economic resources are likely to see the quality of their lives deteriorating systematically without having alternatives. But the national economy, as a whole, will perform at a much lower level than it is capable of doing.

DIFFERENCE BETWEEN DECENTRALIZATION AND STATES' RIGHTS

As opposed to providing the foundation for a complete states' rights atmosphere, where each state functions totally independently from others, it is possible to develop an environment of decentralization. In so doing, federal programs to fulfill national goals can be implemented effectively, and the possible problems stemming from a situation of pure states' rights can be eliminated. Additionally, in implementing national programs, states will use their own preferences and priorities.

Exhibit 6–1 presents a general comparison of states' rights and decentralization, which deals with five specific areas: continuity, opportunity, efficiency, experience and talent. Although Exhibit 6–1 is quite self-explanatory and also the earlier discussions in this book relate to some of these issues, a brief examination of these points is presented for further explanation and elaboration.

- Continuity implies that in many vital areas such as the environmental or education-related issues, the states' rights approach will create discontinuity and a checkered posture. Decentralization, on the other hand, will provide a nationwide application of programs with local nuances and variations.

- Opportunity relates to having the possibility to optimize the national economy as a whole. States' rights are likely to create a situation of suboptimization. However, decentralization, by implementing an overall optimization plan, may prove to have greater possibilities for the national economy to optimize.

- Efficiency is related to input/output relationships. States' rights make it possible for each state to pursue its own economic activity and seek efficiency. However, duplication and significantly different priorities make it nearly impossible for the country to achieve economic efficiency. Decentralization can remedy the situation and lead the country in the direction of efficiency.

- Experience depends upon what individual states have done in terms of public programs from, say, educational to environmental programs. Most states have accomplished very little along these lines. Hence, if left alone, states will be dealing with "trial and error" which could not be in the best interest of consumers. However, in a decentralized situation, the federal experiences can be transplanted to states and adjusted to local needs. Experience particularly in investments with only very long-term payoff possibilities here is very critical. Much of the time states do not invest in basic research. But some states benefit from the outcomes of basic research. If the basic research is successful, many breakthroughs are generated. Then the private sector by using these breakthroughs flourishes.

- Discussion is based on the availability of local talent. Much of the time the best local talent would flee to greener pastures. Therefore, particularly in certain states, good talent may be hard to come by, especially if the states do not have very good talent to develop and administer these important programs. In a decentralization situation, the federal government can share the experienced talent that may be available.

Exhibit 6–1
A General Comparison of States Rights and Decentralization

	STATES' RIGHTS	DECENTRALIZATION
National Continuity in Key Issues	Discontinuity Checkered Posture	Effective implementation of national programs
Opportunity To Optimize	Significantly hindered and reduced	Greater possibility to optimize if the national goals are carefully identified
Efficiency on Implementation	Not likely to be very efficient since each state has its own efficiency capabilities	Likely to be more efficient since it is coordinated
Experience in Initiating and Implementing Unique Projects	Most state programs are primarily pilots and untested	Federal experience can be used to adjust programs to local needs
Availability of Local Talent	Most and best local talent is already moved elsewhere to capitalize on existing opportunities	The lack of local talent can be remedied by appointments from the federal government

Exhibit 6–1 does not present a complete list. However, it makes a strong case for decentralized federalism as opposed to states' rights. The implication here is the choice: centralized federalism, decentralized federalism and states' rights. This point is more clearly illustrated in Exhibit 6–2.

In a democratic market capitalism, there are at least three major alternatives to develop and implement social programs (Exhibit 6-2). Centralized federalism is one extreme. On the other end of the spectrum is states' rights which, in one sense, is economic anarchy. Between these two extremes is a large variety of decentralization of federalism.

The assumption behind Exhibit 6–2 is that if the national imperatives are taken care of and economic goals are fulfilled, consumers' empowerment can yield much more economic wealth than either of the two extremes of the

Exhibit 6–2
Federalism Versus States' Rights

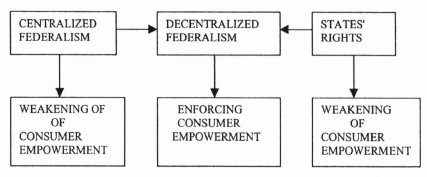

spectrum. However, decentralized federalism does not by definition imply that it will automatically enforce consumer empowerment. It certainly establishes better conditions for a national synergistic economic performance, and possibilities for better empowerment of consumers in general. Here continuity in the programs and the search for a synergistic economic optimization is not hindered by some degree of decentralization in the implementation of programs at the state level. This is substantially different than having each state developing its own agenda and pursuing it without much consideration for a national synergistic economic optimization.

It must be reiterated here that I do not think decentralization means division of the country. Going back to the beginning of this chapter, a decentralized orchestra is still under the conductor's direction as opposed to division, which implies all of the musicians being totally on their own. The following examples, to a certain extent, illustrate the differences between total decentralization that is states' rights versus the decentralized federalism that is advocated here.

- Manufacturing technology centers are part of a national network. They characterize a new model of economic distribution, conventional localism and new federalism. They provide opportunities to decentralize locally while optimizing nationally (Sabel 1996).

- China developed a decentralized federalism and achieved economic growth before experimenting with democracy. Russia, on the other hand, totally decentralized and democratized without any federalism and without making any economic progress (*Business Week* June 7, 1993). So far this has been a total failure.

- The Intermodal Surface Transportation Efficiency Act (ISTEA) (Baker and Ryder 1997) created an illustration of decentralized federalism. However, if it becomes totally decentralized (states' rights) it will succumb to local special interest pressures.

- Lots of proposed program cuts, curbs on grants and de facto devolutions of program responsibilities have all been the results of efforts involved in the extended attempts to enforce states' rights. These attempts caused not assigning certain key functions and letting them to somehow disappear. Among these very functions are: public infrastructure, job training, education reform, housing, rural services and economic development (Walker 1996). While some states took them seriously, many others totally or partially ignored the key functional areas. These would inevitably enhance the consumer empowerment in those states.

The first three examples—manufacturing technology centers, the Chinese experience and ISTEA—are all decentralized federalism. The fourth example reiterates what could happen if an extreme states' rights movement takes over. Many originally federally initiated programs fall through the cracks, including such programs as the development of public infrastructure, job-training, education reform, housing, rural services and economic development.

DECENTRALIZATION DOES NOT MEAN DIVISION

It is maintained here that decentralized federalism—that is, localized and adjusted federal goals and plans—is superior to each state trying to maximize its economic well-being, much of the time at the expense of others. The end result of this type of states' rightsism is a very checkered status of national goals and national well-being. In fact, states' rights pursued with great zeal can accomplish nothing more than national suboptimization. Synergism and national optimal performance cannot be achieved in a divisionistic atmosphere under the big push for states' rights.

States' rights or decentralized federalism do not by definition mean empowerment of the consumer. But if the economy is likely to perform better, the chances of more successful consumer empowerment are significantly enhanced. Since it is maintained here that decentralized federalism is more likely to enhance overall economic performance, it is more desirable for empowering the consumer.

SUMMARY

This chapter first and foremost posits that if the economy is performing at an optimal level, everybody will benefit. The chances of achieving consumer empowerment are greater when the national economy is functioning at its best.

The chapter distinguished federalism from states' rights as the two extreme alternatives of a spectrum. It is maintained here that federalism, if planned and implemented properly, can generate economic synergism. States' rights have been creating checkered and discontinuous situations in most of the national economic issues. However, it is also maintained that in planning and particularly in implementing national economic programs to optimize the performance of the market system, some degree of decentralization to carry out national programs is important. Thus, the chapter makes a case for a decentralized federalism, than rather simply allowing fifty states to totally go their own way.

REFERENCES

Baker, Denise and Ryder, Julienne Ryan (1997). "Panelists Agree: Intermodal Surface Transportation Efficiency Act is Federalism at Its Best," *Nations Cities Weekly*, March 17, 6–7.

Business Week (1993). "The New Federalism: Tonic for World Growth," June 7, 122–123.

Hefner, Frank L. (1997). "Using Input-Output Models to Measure Local Economic Impacts," *International Journal of Public Administration*, August–September, 1469–1488.

Kelly, Kevin and Melcher, Richard A. (1995). "Power to the States," *Business Week*, August 7, 48–56.

Kotler, Philip; Jatusripitak, Somkid; and Maesincee, Suvit (1997). *The Marketing of Nations*. New York: The Free Press.

Sabel, Charles F. (1996). "A Measure of Federalism: Assessing Manufacturing Technology Centers," *Research Policy*, March, 281–308.

Schlesinger, Arthur M., Jr. (1995). "In Defense of Government," *The Wall Street Journal*, June 7, A14.

Smith, Adam (1776). *Inquiry into the Nature and Causes of the Wealth of Nations*, London: George Routledge.

Thurow, Lester C. (1999). *Building Wealth* New York: HarperCollins.

Walker, David B. (1996). "The Advent of an Ambiguous Federalism and the Emergence of New Federalism," *Public Administration Review*, May-June, 271–280.

Chapter 7

Regulation for Competition, Not of Competition

Throughout the chapters of this book, it has been reiterated time and again that competition is the essence of capitalism and that capitalism does and must thrive on the empowerment of consumers. The more competition in the market system, the greater its economic accomplishments. The more consumers participate in these accomplishments of the market system and receive reasonable rewards for their toil, the stronger the stance for capitalism. However, it is difficult to assume that if there were no regulations, guidelines or some direction the market would be bound to go in the right direction, and the economy would function at an optimal level. A certain structure or order must be present for the market system to flourish. In the previous chapter, it was pointed out that if individual states were allowed to function totally independently, there would not be any possibility for the economy to achieve synergism and function at a level of optimal performance. The common stance in recent years has been that if there is deregulation and individual states are left alone to function according to their own preferences, the economy will perform very well. In this context, the key objective of this chapter is to dispel a common misconception that deregulation enhances competition. Deregulation can easily be anticompetition as well as procompetition. It is critical to identify these two diametrically opposing points of view and decide which one and under what circumstances.

DEREGULATION AND COMPETITION

Thurow (1996) posits that capitalism's biggest shortcoming is myopia because it has a very short-term horizon. This is why many dramatic decisions in our society are made without considering the long-term implications. The deregulation movement in the United States started at the end of the Nixon-Ford era, continued during the Carter era and is still on-going. The original idea regarding deregulation is that left alone and unhindered, the market will optimize its economic activity. Again, unhindered, there would be more and keener competition that would help the market to optimize and synergize. Deregulation was assumed to achieve that. However, such an orientation, even if it pays off, is only for the short run. Instead of enhancing competition, deregulation encourages numerous new entrants who soon fail and exit and, more importantly, deregulation sets the stage for the first major wave of merger mania. It has been continuing ever since at an accelerating rate.

The critical consideration here is that deregulation does create competition in the short run but when the dust settles, companies start buying each other off and, hence, they create oligopolies and more monopoly power in the marketplace. Thus, in the long run deregulation is primarily anticompetition.

THE BANKING SECTOR AFTER DEREGULATION

Although deregulation, first and foremost, is designed to enhance competition, in the banking sector, this did not evidence itself. Studies indicated that deregulation did not have a significant impact on the economic efficiency of the U.S. banking industry (Grabowski, Rangon and Rezvanian 1994). Thus, deregulation did not have the positive impact that was expected on competition from the beginning. In fact, the same study posited that after deregulation, the industry's overall effectiveness along with its efficiency of scale and in technical areas have declined (Grabowski et al. 1994). In addition to this questionable start, the number of banks in the United States declined significantly. Whereas in 1985 there were 18,043 banks, this number came down to 15,162 in 1990 and to 11,970 in 1995 (*Statistical Abstract*). This is a very large decline that is due to the merger mania in the banking industry. It was triggered by the deregulation process. Thus, banks have become larger. It has been established that larger banks charge larger fees, they are removed from consumers, and they are neither flexible nor caring. (Please see chapter 2, Appendix B.)

A number of the largest corporations in the United States have realized that the belief that bigger is better is not quite realistic and are abandoning it. AT&T, ITT and EDS decided to break up their organizations and spin off their many businesses. Their decisions were based on strategic objectives rather than financial considerations. These companies are exploring the strategic postures generated by having several independent companies that cannot be well-managed by only one conglomerate (Peltz 1996). However, banks, in general, are far away from this kind of thinking. They still maintain that their mergers are creating economies of scale and their lowered costs due to mergers are a benefit to the American consumer. However, American consumers are paying more and more for less and less. The larger banks are charging more in terms of fees, are paying less in the form of interest and are very limited in catering to the particular needs of their customers. Hence, if the management internally does not solve the problem and live up to its promises, society externally will have to do something drastic such as reregulation. Here immediate financial gains must be evaluated against future performance based on strategic plans and their implication. The long-run market gains and their distribution among the consumers (or the stakeholders) must come first.

AIRLINES AFTER DEREGULATION

Numerous empirical studies dealing with the domestic productivity of the airline industry indicate that deregulation has generated a very complex picture where there is no clear-cut illustration of both economic and industrial benefits due to deregulation (Adrangi, Chow and Raffice 1996). The deregulation activity in this industry led originally to lower fares on busy routes, but service to less heavily traveled cities has become much more expensive or has totally disappeared (Kotler, Jatusripitak and Maesincee 1997). Furthermore, some maintain that those originally lower fares also increased at a faster pace than inflation in American society. Additionally, research into aircraft engine maintenance indicates that there has been a clear reduction in engine maintenance effort after deregulation. However, this trend did not show that there is a tendency toward deterioration in engine performance (Mark 1993). But it cannot be stated that in the long run this will not be a problem. Because of the lack of pressure from the federal government and because of lack of competition, airlines don't seem to be improving their efficiency and catering more and more to consumer needs.

TELEPHONE INDUSTRY—THE DEATH OF MA BELL

The divestiture of AT&T in January 1984 resulted in a smaller and, some maintain, more flexible company. Dividing AT&T into seven regional Bell companies referred to as "baby bells" brought competition into the telecommunications industry, and customers now pay 65 percent less per minute for telephone services. Many observers do not credit the divestiture for many of the improvements that the industry has experienced. Rather, they attribute the rate reductions to the fact that the breakup did reduce AT&T's lobbying power (Kirvan 1994). In recent years, the same industry is in a merger mode. It appears that, deep down, baby bells may agree with the negative point of view and would like to improve the lobbying power and bring it up to what it used to be before the breakup. Certainly, if consumers are paying less for more services, this is a positive step in the path of achieving consumer empowerment. However, if deregulation allows the baby bells to go back to the good old days, then all the benefits are lost.

Banking, airlines, and telephone companies exemplify deregulation. At the point of writing this book, the utility companies, the health care sector and perhaps, above all, the education sector are all embattled by the pros and cons of deregulation and privatization.

THE BIG MEDIA GAME

When Viacom absorbed CBS for $37 billion, it created one of the nine massive conglomerates that have emerged since the mid-1980s to dominate the U.S. media landscape (McChesney 1999). This, McChesney posits, is a growing threat to our republic. Then he cites James Madison: "A popular government without popular information, or the means of acquiring it, is but a prologue to a farce or a tragedy, or perhaps both." The fact is that the extensive concentration of the nine media giants run by some extremely wealthy people may enforce Madison's vision of the American government being run without popular information. Time will tell if this is a farce or a tragedy. But one thing is for sure: if the regulators at the Federal Communications Commission and in the antitrust division of the Justice Department were doing their jobs or if the Telecommunications Act of 1996 were not railroaded through by the U.S. Congress, this oligopolistic devel-

Exhibit 7–1
Aspects of Privatization

Pros	Cons
Stimulates initiative and creativity	Plays up to the greed factor
Encourages efficiency	Unnecessary duplication leading to inefficiency
Contributes to enhancement of competition Creates wealth for some private people or groups	Encouraging collusion or merger Allows too much wealth and power to accumulate in the hands of a few

opment would not have taken place. The air waves don't appear to belong to the people anymore (McChesney 1999).

THE MEANING AND IMPLICATIONS OF PRIVATIZATION

Privatization, in essence, means that an activity, a function or an organization is transferred from the public to the private sector (Kotler, Jatusripitak and Maesincee 1997). It also involves market deregulation and, as such, is strongly related to the well-being and empowerment of consumers. Just why privatize? Exhibit 7–1 presents some key pros and cons of privatization.

Indeed, during the past forty years of academic and professional life, almost all of my acquaintances in Eastern Europe have advocated privatization. At the point of writing this book, ex-communist countries such as the Czech Republic have ministers of privatization. Justifiably or unjustifiably, the majority of the people in these countries believe that privatization will stimulate initiative and creativity. Therefore, bureaucracy and red-tape-laden industries from the communist era will find new life and, by definition, will contribute to the well-being of society. But can we accomplish everything in a society by mobilizing private sources in pursuit of profits? Some extreme thinkers have harped on the virtues of human greed. They maintain that in pursuit of happiness, if left alone, human beings will do the right thing and will accomplish economic well-being. Although this position is very idealistic and admirable, it misses the point of this book. At any given time, people are not equal nor do they have equal access to opportunities. Therefore, it is not realistic to assume that everyone can make the best decisions regarding their choices in an effort to improve their own quality of life. Thus, there is no foundation for leaving everybody alone (deregulation to a point of lawlessness) and assuming that they will all excel in their undertakings. However, on the other hand, given opportunities, those who can probably will strive for greater efficiency under privatization. This situation would further enhance competition in the marketplace and, therefore, all of these factors of privatization would enhance the empowerment of competition.

However, as was mentioned earlier, privatization does not necessarily mean people will excel or that the private sector does things better than the public sector. Furthermore, if and when the private sector achieves a competitive edge and commensurate profits, it does not necessarily mean that those who participate in it will be rewarded proportionately. There is, for instance, an ongoing discussion of the pros and cons of privatization. If privatization achieves savings for an industry, these savings are coming from lower wages or from higher productivity (Allen 1995). To the extent that privatization and deregulation give extraspecial powers to the capitalist top management, there is always the opportunity for exploitation of labor and hence consumers. This is what is meant by the "greed" factor in Exhibit 7–1. There is no reason to assume that, given the opportunity, individuals will choose competitive and productive avenues rather than easy ways to make large profits at the expense of others. The greed factor gives way to exploitation if and when it is possible. In addition to the greed factor, privatization can also cause unnecessary duplication of certain activities, such as too many telephone companies providing the same type of service and, hence, creating inefficiencies that are likely to be costly to consumers. Once such duplication and resultant deterioration of the profit picture set in, the companies facing such a picture are likely to be tempted to get together with competitors, attempt to fix prices, divide the market and practice other anticompetition activities. Although such activities are against the law, it is not easy to detect them and enforce the law to protect consumers.

THE LEGAL CONSTRAINTS

Our discussion thus far brings us to a point that lawlessness does not mean competition. In other words, the law of the jungle should not be construed as the principle that would advance modern capitalism. However, there is evidence that reducing legal barriers can enhance competition. This does not mean that elimination of laws across the board should stimulate competition, which, in turn, will kindle increases in productivity. Elimination of

Exhibit 7–2
The Political Posture Toward Regulation

	Private Life	Market System
Democratic Party	Less Prolegislation	More Prolegislation
Republican Party	More Prolegislation	Less Prolegislation

some laws is likely to lead to reduction in competition, which is a self-defeatist proposition.

Since the laws are connected to the political posture of the country, it is necessary to briefly examine the stance of political parties regarding regulation and deregulation. Unless the political posture of the country is in the direction of maintaining and preferably enhancing competition, there is no possibility for advancing consumers' empowerment in the United States. The two major political parties display dramatically opposing positions regarding laws and regulation (See Exhibit 7–2).

It is very curious that the Republican party, which is extremely antilegislation regarding consumer protection and corporate behavior in the marketplace, is very prolegislation regarding abortion, desecration of the flag, pornography, prayers in schools and the like. Under Republican administrations starting with Ronald Reagan, there has been a deterioration in the enforcement of major U.S. laws that are antimonopoly, such as antitrust laws. In fact, one can easily observe that while the Republican party has been in favor of deregulation in the marketplace, it has been quite trigger happy in regulating abortions, school prayer and the like. The opposite can be stated for the Democratic party. It advocates more regulation in the marketplace and less in the private lives of citizens.

One of the most important points being made here is that unless both political parties understand the importance of consumer empowerment, it will be impossible to make progress in this area. It is equally critical to understand that there are alternative approaches. Thus, it is possible for the two parties to maintain their identity by pursuing different policies to achieve consumer empowerment without deviating from the goal of consumer empowerment, which should be a common goal for both parties.

Perhaps the worst aspect of the legal framework that is applied to the business sector and the market is that different laws have been passed to stop certain practices after the fact and, therefore, all of the activity here has been on a piecemeal basis. However, what is essentially needed is a series of laws that are geared to generating and maintaining a certain level of competition and empowering the consumer. This is a very important point for the future of American capitalism and its success. It will have to take, once again and most emphatically, a nonpolitical and nondoctrinaire approach about a general agreement to maintain a certain level of competition and to empower the American consumer. American capitalism can survive only if such conditions are met. Just what are the key areas where laws can facilitate and enhance competition?

CONDITIONS LEADING TO LAWS THAT WOULD ENHANCE COMPETITION

Exhibit 7–3 presents some of the key conditions that are necessary to maintain competition and create consumer empowerment. Perhaps the most obvious condition is to stop monopolies and all the attempts to monopolize. Some of the most obvious aspects of merger mania need to be stopped. Also when certain firms become too big and monopolize, they must be broken into multiple firms. Although antitrust laws have been dealing with these issues, during the past decade they have not been strenuously enforced.

Creating a monopoly or attempting to create a monopoly is not as common as some firms' creating excessive market power that is monopolistic through certain practices. Practices such as price discrimination and manufacturers' excessive power that is used to keep dealers and distributors in control are strong hindrances to competition and are not quite controlled by legal means. Trade discounts must be fair and available under similar situations to everyone. Otherwise, small retailers cannot compete with large retailers, and small wholesalers cannot compete with large wholesalers.

Although the first two items in Exhibit 7–3 deal with these conditions, it is also necessary to have a catch-all parameter regarding competition. Any attempt that will lessen or hurt competition must be stopped. It is critical also to establish uniform criteria that will not change from state to state and that will be administered and implemented locally. Since attempts to hurt

Exhibit 7–3
Conditions Leading to Laws to Enhance Competition

Principles to Maintain or Enhance Competition	Needs
To stop monopolies or attempt to monopolize	To stop merger mania
To stop practices deliberately trying to create monopoly power	To prevent price discrimination, manufacturers' power over distributors, to enhance fair trade discounts
To stop any attempt to hurt competition	To establish uniform criteria administered and implemented locally to block activities that might hurt competition
To stop individualized state-specific practices that are considered fair trade or fair economic activity but create confusion and inconsistency in other states	To develop and implement across the board fairness in the trade and economic activity
To prohibit economic power or asset acquisition that may hinder competition	To make sure that companies cannot expand their product distribution systems, their communication activity to hinder competition by buying out competitors' assets or expertise
To prevent practices that would mislead consumers and discriminate against them	To establish parameters of fairness that would enable individuals to make better decisions without being misled or exploited

or lessen competition may vary from one locality to another, it is critical to provide local flexibility within the prescribed guidelines.

At the same time, individualized state-specific practices that are considered "fair" may vary so much from one state to another that they may create confusion and inconsistency. Thus, across the board, fairness in dealing with competition and the well-being of consumers must be reexamined, and certain general criteria must be established so that fairness in the trade within and between states will always be present.

Companies must be using their economic power not to acquire assets or the economic power of others but to develop new methods, new techniques, new products. Finally, Exhibit 7–3 posits that certain practices that would mislead consumers or discriminate against them in different ways must be prevented. This will call for establishing parameters of fairness that would enable individual consumers to make better decisions without being misled or exploited.

Exhibit 7–3 does not necessarily present an exhaustive list. It certainly does not imply the need for many more laws that may hinder good decisions and stifle initiative. However, certain behaviors on the part of the business sector are described through the conditions specified in Exhibit 7–3. If such behaviors do not materialize, the market system cannot possibly empower consumers and enhance their quality of life.

SUMMARY

If consumer empowerment is a necessary condition for the market system to perform well, then competition must be maintained and enhanced. Deregulation does not, by definition, mean competition. On the contrary, it encourages unnecessary and counterproductive mergers that limit the power of consumers. This chapter attempts to illustrate that deregulation and its cohort privatization are not likely to generate the results once envisioned. Rather, there must be regulation to maintain and enhance competition. Six key conditions are presented in this chapter, the presence of which is essential for competition to get stronger. These conditions will necessitate looking at the legal structure again carefully. The laws should not be passed piecemeal but should be there to fulfill the overall objective of competition, leading to consumer empowerment.

REFERENCES

Adrangi, Bahram; Chow, Garland; and Raffice, Kambiz (1996). "Passenger Output and Labor Productivity in the U.S. Airline Industry After Deregulation: A Profit Function Approach," *The Logistics and Transportation Review*, December, 389–408.

Allen, Michael (1995). "Pro and Con: An Ardent Advocate of Privatization Squares off Against a Staunch Opponent," *Wall Street Journal*, Oct. 2, R27.

Grabowski, Richard; Rangon, Nanda; and Rezvanian, Rasoul (1994). "The Effect of Deregulation on the Efficiency of U.S. Banking Firms," *Journal of Economics and Business*, February, 39–55.

Kirvan, Paul F. (1994). "Divestiture: Its Impact on End-Users (AT&T Breakup 10 Years Later)," *Communication News*, January, 11–14.

Kotler, Philip; Jatusripitak, Somkid; and Maesincee, Suvit (1997). *The Marketing of Nations*. New York: The Free Press.

Mark, Kenneth D. (1993). "Did Deregulation Affect Aircraft Engine Maintenance? An Empirical Policy Analysis," *Rand Journal of Economics*, Winter, 542–551.

McChesney, Robert W. (1999). "Oligopoly: The Big Media Game Has Fewer Players," *The Progressive*, November, 20–24.

Peltz, Michael (1996). "Breaking Up Is Tempting to Do," *Institutional Investor*, January, 60–62.

Statistical Abstract of the United States (various years). Washington, DC, Department of Commerce.

Thurow, Lester C. (1996). *The Future of Capitalism*. New York: William Morrow.

The Workings of a Mixed Economy

No economy can be pure. The USSR was not a purely communist system. The United States is not a purely capitalist system. In fact, it is not possible to have a purely government-controlled or a purely private economy. The key question here is: just what kind of combination of public and private sectors would be most desirable?

Many years ago, John Kenneth Galbraith (1967) stated that a larger world was beginning to obtrude in his thoughts:

> This was a world of great corporations in which people increasingly served the convenience of these organizations which were meant to serve them. It was a world in which the motives of organization members seemed not to fit the standard textbook mold. Nor did the relationship between business and state. Nor did markets. Especially markets. So far from being the controlling power in the economy, markets were more and more accommodated to the needs and convenience of business organizations (p. vii).

This quotation is extremely critical because the conditions described by Galbraith are not only present today, some thirty-three years later, but are even more pronounced.

The American economy is a combination of private and public sectors, connected and modified by markets. But if the markets are not strong enough, or, as stated throughout this book, if the American consumers are not empowered, then the economy is not likely to function as beneficially as it could for the whole country. In other words, the American economy is a mixed economy of private and public sectors and their balance is of the utmost importance. If these two sectors are in balance optimally, then the American economy performs well and consumers' empowerment is, if not complete, at least in the right direction. But if they are not properly balanced, the economy would perform less than optimally and the tyranny that was discussed earlier will be more of a reality. This chapter explores the balance between these two sectors and examines the direction of interaction between them.

ESTABLISHING THE PARAMETERS

There are no magical formulas regarding the relationship between private and public sectors. Is there a ratio that would optimize society's economic well-being and empower American consumers? This is an extremely important but totally unanswered question. Instead, Republicans keep on saying that we, as a society, need smaller government, and Democrats are trying to hold the line and keep the government approximately as is. In either case, the emphasis is on the size of the government as opposed to the functions and performance of the government. Regardless of which party is in power, these two dogmatic orientations are not likely to provide the necessary optimization of private and public sectors.

It must be carefully articulated that private and public sectors are not *substitutes*. Rather, they complement each other. This complementary relationship, if utilized carefully, is very synergistic. The synergy that is created by developing proper parameters for private and public sectors invariably benefits the whole society and particularly all consumers.

In order for the proposed synergism to materialize, the whole process of establishing the parameters of the mixed economy must begin at the consumer level in society. By starting at that level, it is possible to identify more accurately what each sector must perform so that society will be better off. Consider, for instance, the following:

- About 40 percent of U.S. bridges are rated deficient.
- An average of 120 American bridges collapse each year, some basi-

cally because they did not receive a new coat of paint and were not protected against the elements.

- Americans waste much time in traffic jams, estimated at around 2 billion hours annually and predicted to double by the year 2005.
- It is estimated that water mains and sewers across the country are reaching the end of their 80 to 100-year life spans (Wieman 1993).

One specific episode can illustrate the seriousness of the problem. In the spring of 1992, in Chicago, 250 million gallons of water poured into a century-old tunnel under the city's central loop. This forced 200,000 people to evacuate. It disrupted state, national and even international business. The city had failed to invest $10,000 in repairing a small underground leak that caused a loss to companies and taxpayers of more than $1 billion in emergency response, property damage and lost business (Wieman 1993).

Yesterday's shortsightedness can cause today's infrastructure crisis. But while the private versus public debate continues, American society is losing much money; but more importantly, it is losing the areas of productivity and synergism that would generate a more productive and economically balanced society (Mudge 1996). Thus, the first principle of a mixed economy is to establish the parameters of the extent to which private and public sectors are going to be given power and budgets on the basis of the infrastructure's needs. The seriousness of the problem does not allow posturizing for political power. However, despite a consensus on the desirability of redeveloping the nation's transportation and communications infrastructure, there is total disagreement as to whether this is a private or public matter and, hence, there is inadequate progress in this extremely important area (Harrison 1993).

If the growing population wants to maintain the level of public services, both urban infrastructure and current services must be increased (Brueckner 1996). Financing such infrastructure costs is quite difficult; however, it must be understood that if the infrastructure is not built adequately and is not maintained, then the cost to society will increase much more than proportionately. Bureaucracy, lack of funds and subsequent lack of professional and skilled public employees are the key factors in this deficiency in infrastructure expansion and maintenance (Wieman 1993). Unfortunately, at the writing of this book the overall discussion revolves around just how much of the tax surpluses should be given back to the people instead of considering serious issues such as infrastructure maintenance and improvement. In other words, the short-term political expediency is being put way ahead of the future health of our economy.

Other aspects of infrastructure are communication, education, energy supply and environmental protection. More will be said about these in chapters 10 and 11. This list certainly can be expanded or shortened. Furthermore, there are no indications as to the relative importance of these various aspects of the infrastructure. In other words, we don't quite know to which aspects of the infrastructure we must pay attention first. This situation poses an additional challenge of determining how much emphasis and effort must be put on each of these key factors. Since society does not have endless resources, it becomes critical to determine the best combination of emphasis for optimal results. It is critical to reiterate that infrastructure development is a cost factor and not profitable. Hence, the private sector does not do enough of it. But, because the private sector does not like to pay taxes either, the public sector cannot do enough to bring the infrastructure up to the necessary par to create the synergism that the whole society can use and benefit from. If the infrastructure is not in place and up to par, then the private sector cannot flourish and be very productive, and the whole society loses. It is not possible to create the desired consumer empowerment under such circumstances.

THE COST OF EQUAL OPPORTUNITY

As mentioned earlier, consumer empowerment leads to equal opportunity. In a mixed economy, both private and public sectors must make an effort to accomplish this goal. At least four key areas are critical here: the *infrastructure, human resource training, competition* and *consumerism*. The infrastructure is discussed in chapter 11, human resource development is discussed in chapter 10, and consumerism is discussed in chapter 12. In addition to financing the infrastructure, which requires substantial outlays up front, creating and maintaining equal opportunity has other substantial cost factors in the short run. As has been mentioned throughout this book, competition is the essence for empowering the consumer. It must be maintained at any cost. The only aspect of this topic that is examined here is the cost of maintaining competition. At least up front and in the short run, maintaining competition can be costly. This is the cost of the investment we make for our future.

Maintaining Competition

In maintaining competition, at least two types of cost must be considered: cost related to merger mania and cost related to business failure. Although each will take much detailed explanation, only a brief description of the situation is presented here.

In various chapters, up to now, merger mania has been discussed in different contexts; in most cases, it has been discussed in a negative light. Much of the time it reduces competition rather than enhancing it. As discussed in different sections of the book, merger mania basically is very harmful to the economy and consumer well-being, since it has unwarranted ability to allocate economic power into the hands of few and create market power imbalances.

However, there are special circumstances under which mergers can also be advantageous. Some research has indicated that economies of scale, scope and speed are all real and could make a difference in enhancing the competitive edge of merging companies (Kotler, Jatusripitak and Maesincee 1997). Thus, stopping forthcoming mergers is not a simple task. The benefit of stopping a forthcoming merger must exceed its negative impact before this can be done. If its negative impact on the economy, competition and the society's well-being is excessive, then the merger must be stopped. However, some benefits will be forgone so that competition can be maintained. At the point of this writing, there are no specified formulas or even concerted efforts to determine the net impact of each merger activity. The antitrust division of the Department of the Justice appears to be more whimsical rather than scientific. It further appears to be more politically driven rather than concerned with economic realities. Therefore, preventing some of the merger activity, which is rather critical because of obvious attempts to limit competition, is likely to have, at least in the short run, a cost impact. This cost is needed to be absorbed for the benefit of maintaining competition in the long run.

Enhancing Competition

Promoting equal opportunity is closely related to entrepreneurship and formation of new businesses. During the past decade and a half, more small service and retail establishments have entered the American market. Similarly, a very large proportion of these new businesses have failed (Samli 1993). A number of factors caused this rather sad outcome.

First, they were easier businesses to start. They took a minimal amount of capital and were low-cost operations.

Second, many people who are trained and educated for positions in large U.S. companies could not get jobs or were downsized and forced to opt to start this type of small firm.

Third, unavailability of venture capital created a major hindrance to start small-to-medium-size technical firms with substantially more capital needs.

Fourth, people with high levels of technical training and education found high-paying jobs easily in highly technical large companies primarily engaged in research for the armed forces or related industries. Thus, small independent, technical firms did not emerge as a part of the business population.

Fifth, the lack of capital combined with the declining supply of highly trained technical labor force contributed to the lack of an emerging technical firm group.

In other words, they could not survive because they lacked the necessary background (Samli 1993 p. 22).

In addition to the large number of failures, the number of small service and retail establishments decreased per thousand of population, indicating that small firms cannot easily hold their own in the modern free markets. Perhaps they fail because they are too small or too inadequate to begin with.

One of the truly misunderstood phenomena in modern market economies is business failure. Perhaps the key reason for this misunderstanding stems from the logic of classical economics. If the market is perfectly competitive, as Adam Smith or Alfred Marshall advocate, then the weak and inefficient will fail. According to classicists, this process will make the economy stronger and more efficient. However, as discussed in this book, the U.S. economy is far away from Adam Smith's or Alfred Marshall's perfectly competitive market (Samli 1993).

If the economy is imperfectly competitive or not at all competitive in that it is composed of oligopolies and monopolies, then the classical assumption that failures will improve the economy must be rejected. Since it is very likely that in modern economies small and very efficient firms can easily fail in less than perfectly competitive markets, business failures are not necessarily beneficial. If more efficient, competitive and versatile firms are failing rather than the weak and less competent firms, then society is not gaining anything. Indeed, in our current market economy, which is not perfect competition, many firms that are run efficiently can and do go out of existence when business conditions are adverse. On the other hand, very large firms, even though not efficient and not well managed, can survive adversities in the marketplace because of their vast resources, that allow them to survive a very lean time in markets that are not totally friendly.

Thus, while in perfect competition the survival of the fittest doctrine can be advanced, in less than perfect competition this doctrine becomes survival of the fattest, indicating that the firm survives not because it is efficient and profitable but because it has large financial resources. These resources enable it to survive the adversities of recession. These businesses can live off the fat they already have (Samli 1993, p. 23).

Because failures in less than perfectly competitive economies may not make a contribution to the overall economy, their cost could be extremely high. Thus intercepting business failures may be beneficial.

Maintaining competition is extremely critical for consumer empowerment, but efforts in this direction are likely to be costly. This cost must be well understood and accounted for. Trying to maintain competition will lead to many business failures, and this is the critical factor behind cost considerations. Exhibit 8–1 indicates that in 1997 there were over 83,000 business failures and more than 54,000 business bankruptcies. The cost of these failures and bankruptcies to society is very high. Although these failures and bankruptcies are somewhat cyclical in that when the economy is doing well, their numbers go down, in absolute terms they are too numerous and, hence, their impact is far reaching. The cost of business failure can be analyzed in two categories: (1) direct costs, and (2) indirect costs. Although business failures and business bankruptcies are not the same, the same type of cost analyses are applicable to both.

Exhibit 8–2 displays the cost implications of business failures and bankruptcies. A brief description of these cost implications is presented in the following sections.

DIRECT COST OF BUSINESS FAILURES

There are at least four specific areas where the costs of business failures are most critical: direct cost to creditors, direct cost of the legal process, cost of lost savings and, most important, cost of the proprietor's time and effort (Exhibit 8–2).

Cost to Creditors: In both small and big business failures, creditors lose substantial sums. These losses have two components. First, creditors lose money that might have at least been used for consumption that would have improved these creditors' quality of life. But more important, they might have used these monies in more profitable ventures that might have created further economic gains. Thus, the cost of failures can be rather excessive to creditors, expressed in terms of lost opportunities or quality of life.

Exhibit 8-1
Business Failures and Bankruptcies, 1990–97

Year	GNP (In Millions of $)	Business Failures	Business Bankruptcy filed	Unemployed (in thousands)	Unemployment Rate
1990	5,513,800	60,568	64,688	6,874	5.5
1991	5,672,600	87,592	64,714	8,426	7.0
1992	6,255,200	97,069	72,650	9,613	7.5
1993	6,563,500	86,133	66,428	8,940	6.9
1994	6,931,900	71,558	56,748	7,996	6.1
1995	7,246,700	71,194	51,288	7,404	5.6
1996	7,567,100	71,931	53,549	7,236	5.4
1997	8,060,100	83,384	54,027	6,739	5.0

Source: Statistical Abstract of the United States, various issues.

Exhibit 8–2
Direct and Indirect Costs of Business Failures

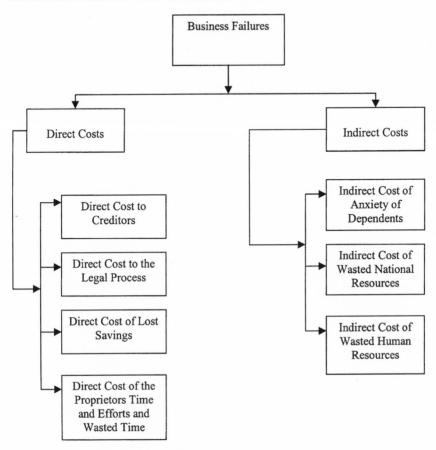

The Cost of Legal Process: Much time and effort goes into the settlement process. All of this is counterproductive in that there is no new productivity or production to show for this wasted time and effort. Not only those who are directly involved in this legal process, but the whole society suffers.

Time and Effort: In addition to losing their lifetime savings as businesses fail, proprietors and workers waste substantial amounts of time and energy until they find other employment. Much of the time the employment they find is not in their area of specialty. Thus the individuals as well as the society lose.

INDIRECT COST OF BUSINESS FAILURES

Exhibit 8–2 illustrates three indirect cost factors. The anxiety of the dependents of those who lost their businesses or their jobs because of business failures is a substantial indirect cost. Not only are their lives disrupted, but also the lives of their dependents are put on hold (Samli 1993). The dependents, instead of pursuing careers or continuing their education, may be forced to take menial jobs that would be counterproductive for the development and the future of the dependents. All of this adds up to a major mass of human as well as capital resources that are wasted. This could be a very large cost factor nationally.

Finally, the human resource waste over and beyond unemployment, idleness and anxiety is a powerful factor to consider. There is a total cost of human resources that is attached to business failures. Business failures could tie up a very valuable, innovative and proactive portion of the labor force. And thus, the society gets much less than what it needs from this talented and unused group.

Exhibit 8–3 reiterates the fact that societal emphasis on entrepreneurial activity, though necessary for consumer empowerment, is very costly because it leads to increased business failures. But these can be entrepreneurial advancement without the emerging large number of small businesses. This increasing number, by definition, creates also an increase in business failures which is very costly.

While society tries to encourage entrepreneurs to generate new businesses, there must be attempts to reduce the number and resultant cost of business failures. There are at least two key weapons to reduce business failures. First, there could be antibusiness failure insurance. Although there are a few programs in this area, none truly is designed to make a dent in the number of business failures. Second is training entrepreneurs so that they will be more successful in their managerial activities. This particular feature is connected to the human resource development that is discussed in chapter 10.

EQUAL OPPORTUNITY AND BUSINESS FAILURES

If we want to empower the American consumer, individuals must have an opportunity to choose among many products and services. Similarly, consumers also must be in a position to start their own businesses and pursue their dreams. These two conditions, if not carefully managed, are costly

Exhibit 8–3
Cost of Empowerment Because of Business Failures

| Societal emphasis on entrepreneurship | → | Emerging large number of small businesses | → | An increase in business failures | → | Additional cost of empowerment |

propositions. However, no matter how costly, they cannot be as harmful as the deterioration of competition as a result of accumulation of economic wealth in the hands of the few. This last condition is deterioration, if not elimination, of competition that shakes the capitalist market system from its roots and creates a terrorist system against the consumer. Thus, instead of being the focal point of the system, consumers are treated as the enemy of the system. They are not to be allowed to gain power and opportunity to enhance their quality of life.

This may be seen as an extreme position. However, any study of world history will illustrate that if society allows the creation of a very large underclass that is experiencing poverty, and a very small upper class that is extremely well off, there will be, sooner or later, a class war. This is the worst scenario for capitalism, but with unchecked markets that lack a concerted effort to empower the consumer, such eventuality is not at all unlikely. It has been posited throughout this book that every effort toward empowering the consumer will be, first, a major step toward elimination of the possibility of a class war and, second, an effort to raise the total economy to a higher plateau wherein everyone in society will have a more elevated economic quality of life.

Just what are the parameters? How much could society spend on consumer empowerment? The answers to these two very complex questions lie in society's orientation to the issue at hand. A society may approach consumer empowerment as a cost item or as an investment into the society's future.

INVESTING INTO SOCIETY'S FUTURE

If we were to take almost 300 million hard-working, well-meaning, reasonably well-trained and educated people together and ask them to pursue their own goals and economic happiness, would society truly accomplish as much as it possibly could? The reader may refer to chapter 6. It is maintained here that 300 million people, haphazardly pursuing their affairs selfishly, are not likely to create the best performance level for themselves as well as society. Many in pursuit of their own well-being may be in the way of others. Thus there would be much activity reflecting some people's efforts nullifying other's efforts. In such cases, there may not even be a net gain for the economy as a whole. And if there is, it may be in favor of the few rich and powerful rather than for the whole society.

However, if the cost of equal opportunity is considered to be an investment for the future, then society provides itself an optimal route for progress to be performed by the market system. This is what Galbraith (this author believes) meant by the market being the *controlling* power. If the market is composed of a highly diffused power of suppliers and similarly extensively diffused power of consumers, then the balanced power would move the market to a higher economic plateau. This is the first stage in optimizing the market economy. Simultaneously, the mixed economy's efforts to develop the infrastructure further would yield optimal results for society as a whole and the consumer in particular. This is the second stage in optimizing the market economy.

The first phase of developing the market by a balanced power of suppliers and demanders can be accomplished only by performing certain tasks. On the supply side maintaining competition, on the demand side providing consumer protection, consumer information and consumer education will accomplish the first phase mentioned above. If this phase is not completed, society stagnates or even goes backward.

The second phase is the development of the infrastructure that is most suitable for the business sector to flourish and perform well in the market by taking care of consumer needs and by empowering them. This is truly investing in society's future. But it is not simply a formula for doing good. If society does not provide for these two phases—that is, first, generating and maintaining competition through diffused power and, second, developing the infrastructure for optimal growth of the private sector—society will end up in two extremely difficult and dangerous situations: the generational conflict and class wars.

THE GENERATIONAL CONFLICT

When the Social Security system was established, the age limit of sixty-five was almost a fraction of 1 percent in the society. For this small number, all the working people in the country made a contribution. Thus, for a while retirement was easy and not an economic burden. However, recently age sixty-five and above has been one of the fastest growing population sectors. Hence, it is becoming a major burden to the economy unless those who are working are making reasonable sums to defray this burden. If the younger generation is supporting a large older generation at an extreme cost to itself, the cost of having this heavy burden will create conflict between operations. Such a generational conflict, in time, may create class wars in society.

The economic burden of supporting larger groups of older citizens can easily create political conflicts in favor of the younger working people. Thus, such a conflict can worsen the economic well-being of older citizens. The situation contributes further to the existing economic dichotomy of having an upper class and a lower class in the market. Such a dichotomy sooner or later leads to class conflicts and ends up in class wars. Most of the civil wars in the history of the world have been based on such adversarial imbalances as seen in the French, Russian and Chinese revolutions. Unchecked and unremedied history repeats its errors.

ESTABLISHING A BALANCE IN THE MIXED ECONOMY

The contents of this chapter provide a direction for the market system to establish a balance between public and private sectors. Such a balance must primarily be based on at least two extremely critical criteria: maintaining competition, and improving the infrastructure to enhance the effectiveness of competition. The market, as brought up at the beginning of this chapter, must be the controlling power in the economy to accommodate to the needs, first and foremost, of consumers in a nondiscriminating manner. If the market were given such power and responsibility, it would carry a certain level of competition. But then, such a level of competition may not be able to be accomplished unless the infrastructure is improving. This basic proposition, that the market must be the controlling power, cannot be achieved without implementing these two conditions. However, if the mixed economy works well, it would bring the optimal economic well-being to all, while also maximizing the profits of the business sector.

SUMMARY

This chapter presents the key considerations regarding the optimal performance of a mixed economy. It points out that markets, instead of being the controlling factor, are accommodating to the convenience of the corporate entity. However, unless private and public sectors are in balance, it will not be possible for the economy to optimize and empower consumers in the way it should be. Such a balance provides synergism to the whole economy.

The chapter posits that, in order to create a balance between private and public sectors leading to economic synergism, improving the infrastructure is one key element that must be taken very seriously and implemented deliberately. Then, it articulates how maintaining competition and the resultant equal opportunity can be costly, particularly in the short run. Here the key cost factor is business failures. Maintaining competition leads to a large number of business failures that are very costly. But the generated synergism, based on improving infrastructure and maintaining competition, would easily outstrip the cost of maintaining competition.

REFERENCES

Brueckner, Jan K. (1996). "A New Way to Finance Urban Infrastructure," *Illinois Business Review*, Fall, 8–11.

Galbraith, J. Kenneth (1967). *The New Industrial State*. Boston: Houghton Mifflin.

Harrison, Bennett (1993). "Making Inroads on Infrastructure," *Technology Review*, April, 70–71.

Kotler, Philip; Jatusripitak, Somkid; and Maesincee, Suvit (1997). *The Marketing of Nations*. New York: The Free Press.

Mudge, Richard A. (1996). "Infrastructure Investment Can Stimulate Growth—An Interview," *Challenge*, March–April, 4–9.

Samli, A. Coskun (1993). *Counterturbulence Marketing*. Westport, CT: Quorum Books.

Wieman, Clark (1993). "Road Work Ahead: How to Solve the Infrastructure Crisis," *Technology Review*, January, 42–49.

_____ **Chapter 9**

Macro and Micro Economic Growth Strategies

Our discussion thus far reiterates that although having ambitious individuals pursuing their economic well-being by working hard in our market system is the most critical ingredient for economic growth, it is not quite sufficient. It is also necessary to provide the proper setting in which individuals can proceed in the direction of improving their economic quality of life.

Providing this proper setting is not something that happens all by itself. As discussed in the previous chapter, our economy is composed of private and public sectors. The mixture of these two components must be just right so that consumers in society will have, first, equal opportunity and, second, a greater probability to succeed as consumers, as workers, as decision-makers—in other words, as citizens. Thus, corporate and government responsibilities need to be identified and critically evaluated. This chapter explores these two sets of responsibilities, ties them to the economy, and examines critically what else is needed to be done toward the empowerment of the American consumer. It is maintained here that both business and government can pursue economic growth strategies jointly. These strategies, if successful, will enhance consumer empowerment.

CORPORATE RESPONSIBILITIES

Throughout our discussion in the previous chapters, we have alluded to the fact that the corporate entity or the private sector in our economy has major responsibilities. These go way beyond just making money. In recent years, many social thinkers and critics have attempted to distinguish between corporate social performance (CSP) and corporate financial performance (CFP), indicating that the private sector's responsibilities are expanding.

During that time period, there have been many attempts to examine the relationship between CSP and CFP. In 1962, Milton Friedman stated that "a corporation's social responsibility is to make a profit" (1970). This started a large-scale debate. Although numerous researchers have explored the relationship between CSP and CFP, there is no definitive consensus on the methodology employed, criteria used and the results obtained (Griffin and Mahon 1997). But in most of these research endeavors, the focus of attention has been on rather less important factors such as "potential corporate illegalities such as antitrust suits" or "problems such as product recalls." Reflecting the attempts to identify the relationship between CSP and CFP, the literature identifies at least four key measures:

1. A totally perceptual measure coined the fortune reputation survey;
2. A hybrid measure of perceptual and multiple dimensions of Kinder, Lyndenberg and Domini, which is known as the KLD index;
3. A purely numerical measure of Toxic Release Inventory which is known as the TRI; and
4. Corporate Philanthropy (Griffin and Mahon 1997).

The results have been very inconclusive, however; at the point of writing this book, companies such as IBM, General Motors and Microsoft are sending out brochures to prospective applicants promoting their companies' philanthropic and environmental programs and, hence, are using social responsibility issues as a tool to recruit human resources (Turban and Greening 1997).

But philanthropic activities and environmental programs are not enough. Lekachmon (1982) many years ago suggested that "economic failure is as much a corporate product as past successes" (p. xv), indicating the macro role of the corporate entity. But this point is not clearly articulated. Simultaneously, negative propaganda about the role of the federal government in the national economy by those who are not quite familiar with the workings of the complex economy (Thomas 1999) makes it difficult for the public sector to perform its most critical functions.

Although stakeholder activists are demanding greater public accountability of a company's social performance, this type of pressure does not enhance a proactive orientation on the part of the business sector.

Businesses must recognize the importance of the proactive stance that has surfaced throughout this book on different occasions. The critical point about this stance is that if 45 million Americans were to have medical care coverage, all medical care providers would make more money. Similarly, if the lowest 20 percent of the lowest income consumer groups were to earn as much as the middle-class income earners, all businesses in the United States, bar none, would benefit, since there would be so much more income and related increase in demand for goods and services. Thus the business sector must take the position of trying to generate more employment, more consumer income and, above all, more consumer value, knowing full well that these will yield greater profits for the firm. (More on these points in chapter 12.)

Indeed, Drucker (1999) maintains that American corporations are in the business of generating wealth. Certainly this cannot be accomplished if they are preoccupied with cost cutting and downsizing. There is a big difference between the positions of Friedman and Drucker. Making a profit per se does not necessarily imply creation of wealth. In pursuit of profits many companies may not even replenish what they take out of the environment and/or the society (Drucker 1999). However, it must be stated here that even generating net wealth is not quite enough. How this wealth could be distributed and how it will enhance consumer empowerment are still issues that need to be scrutinized very carefully. This point is originally made in chapter 1 as Exhibit 1–1 is discussed. That exhibit almost by definition identifies the areas of corporation that are necessary for the society to achieve all it can.

GOVERNMENT'S RESPONSIBILITIES

In the previous chapter, the workings of a mixed economy are discussed. It is posited that both private and the public sectors must be balanced so that society can make optimal progress. In this chapter, one additional point is presented. The two sectors should not only be in balance but must also strive for excellence so that society can optimize its economic endeavors.

On the part of the government, having an adequate infrastructure in its broadest sense, with education, communication and energy provisions, is not quite enough. It is necessary for the government to help set up the conditions for those key industries that will benefit society in the most desirable manner. That simply means that those industries that create the most well-paying jobs and that generate the largest economic wealth while being environmentally neutral or even positive—that is, that will not create pollution or that may even reduce pollution—will receive support to flourish.

DOMESTIC GROWTH STRATEGIES

If we combine the topics of corporate responsibilities and government responsibilities, then domestic growth strategies can be identified. This concept is based on the economic multiplier principle (Keynes 1935; Dillard 1948). The late Lord Keynes developed his theory of employment primarily on effective demand, which states that employment depends on the total sum of expenditures, both on consumption and investment. Of these two, investment depends on the marginal efficiency of capital, and consumption depends on the size of consumer net income and their propensity to consume (Dillard 1948; Keynes 1936). A high propensity to consume, which is the tendency to purchase on the part of consumers in a society, is a strong stimulant for employment and resultant economic growth in a society. The higher the propensity to consume, the larger the multiplier that makes the economy grow further and more than proportionately in terms of what is originally invested. For instance, if marginal consumption (the last additional unit of consumption) is 80 units and income is 100 units, then marginal propensity to consume is 8–10, and the multiplier is 100/20, which is 5. If the propensity to consume goes from 8/10 to 9/10, then the multiplier becomes 100/10, which is 10. This means when the multiplier was 5, just one dollar of investment would have yielded five dollars in total income. However, when the multiplier is increased and becomes 10, the increase in the income, due to a larger multiplier, will be ten dollars for each dollar invested. Thus, the higher the propensity to consume, the greater the multiplier. Accordingly, investing in different industries does not generate the same multiplier. Different industries generate different levels of income, or in other words investment in different industries would generate different levels of wealth.

Exhibit 9–1 illustrates how economic opportunities can be created by facilitating the activities of those industries that will make the greatest contribution to the economy. As seen in the exhibit, this is a joint activity between the private and public sectors. Again it is based on the premise that all industries do not contribute to the economy equally. In other words, they

Exhibit 9–1
Generating Greater Opportunities in the Marketplace

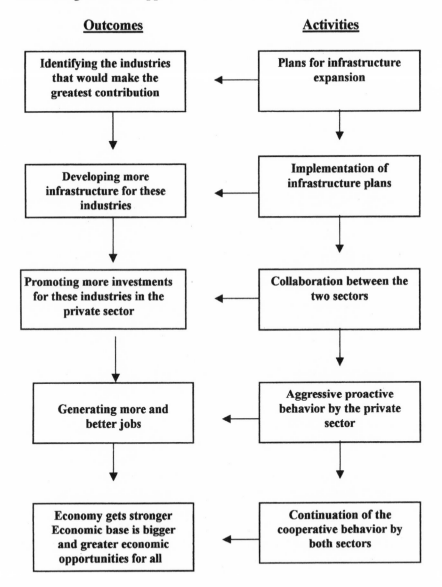

Outcomes	Activities

Identifying the industries that would make the greatest contribution ← **Plans for infrastructure expansion**

Developing more infrastructure for these industries ← **Implementation of infrastructure plans**

Promoting more investments for these industries in the private sector ← **Collaboration between the two sectors**

Generating more and better jobs ← **Aggressive proactive behavior by the private sector**

Economy gets stronger Economic base is bigger and greater economic opportunities for all ← **Continuation of the cooperative behavior by both sectors**

have different economic multipliers and they can generate different levels of wealth.

The first set of activities is related to making plans and implementing them toward improving the infrastructure for the expansion of industries that would make the greatest contribution to the growth of the economy. As industrial expansion and further development are contemplated, the public and private sectors must work together to optimize economic benefits, for any industry that is targeted for expansion can expand successfully only when the infrastructure is adequate. However, much of the time, development of the infrastructure is costly and not profitable. Building a major public high-way, for instance, that may be necessary to move products, costs millions of dollars and yet does not directly yield any money unless toll fees are collected from those who use the highway, which would take a very long time, if at all feasible.

Once these industries flourish partially because of the improved infrastructure, they generate many more high-paying jobs. Of course, as discussed in macro economic books, multipliers create a ripple effect. There are waves of growth created by the first wave, which is directly attributable to the improved infrastructure and original investment in those chosen industries. Certainly, generating more and better jobs is the outcome of the aggressive and proactive behavior of these industries. As a result, as seen in Exhibit 9–1, the economy gets stronger, its base gets bigger and, of course, these optimal circumstances yield greater economic opportunities for all.

This is a very proactive approach to creating optimal economic conditions that would benefit all. Perhaps the most important point that needs to be reiterated is that the proper collaboration of private and public sectors generates optimal conditions for the economy. Those optimal conditions are not likely to materialize without the necessary collaboration. But the private sector's proactive behavior is also essential. Here a growth and expansion strategy is essential for the desired results. Those who believe that the market has supernatural powers and can do this if left totally free must be reminded of the experiences of the Great Depression. The market can simply sink through a downward spiral if a recession begins and, as it sinks deeper, it gets into a depression if nothing is done about it. Thus private and public sectors are both needed to create greater opportunities for all. They must counteract this trend before it is too late. Of course, as implied in Exhibit 9–1, this is not simply a one-time proposition that takes place only in recessions. To enable consumers to reach out and pursue their economic happiness, the process must continue indefinitely.

It must be reiterated that this whole process is geared to stakeholder-activist operations that would enhance the economy and the stakeholders' well-being. It is maintained here that all consumers are stakeholders in a society. Even the stockholders are stakeholders as well and hence they cannot lose sight of this very important point. However, mismanagement of activist issues will certainly result in lost markets and revenues. These lost markets and revenues are depicted by a decrease in stock prices, very large legal and medical fees, costly management compensation and unproductive management time (Downing 1997). This domestic growth picture also has an international counterpart. In the accelerating speed of globalization, America cannot ignore the opportunities and challenges that this process brings about.

INTERNATIONAL GROWTH STRATEGIES

Thurow (1993) indicated that unlike what we have experienced during the second half of the twentieth century, international trade in the twenty-first century will have a considerably different impact. Whereas during the second half of the twentieth century all parties that were involved in international trade benefited, in the twenty-first century, only some will benefit. In other words, the international trade is changing from a win-win to a win-lose situation (Thurow 1993). This distinction between the second half of the twentieth century and the first half of the twenty-first century is attributable to the switch from comparative advantage to competitive advantage (Samli and Jacobs 1995).

According to the comparative advantage doctrine, countries are not equally endowed with natural resources. Furthermore, they have different temperaments and different skills. As a result, some countries can produce certain products less expensively. This implies that other countries will be better off importing these products rather than producing them themselves. Hence, these countries can emphasize the goods and services that they can produce more economically. Thus, everyone is involved in trade and they are all better off. This is a win-win situation (Samli and Jacobs 1995).

However, in the early 1990s a new concept of international trade emerged. This was named the competitive advantage (Porter 1990; Thurow 1993; Samli and Jacobs 1995). Whereas the comparative advantage is related to better utilization of national resources and capabilities, the competitive advantage focuses on managerial expertise and proactive implementation of sophisticated strategic plans (Porter 1990; Samli and Jacobs 1995; Jatusripitak et al. 1989). But the critical point here is that whereas trade that is based on comparative advantage is conceptualized to be a win-win situation for all participating parties, trade based on competitive advantage is conceptualized to be a win-lose proposition. According to economic thinking, comparative advantage in time reaches a level of equilibrium whereby all participants receive equal pay for their resources that are being traded. However, in competitive advantage, these countries and/or companies can continue making much more than their trading partners because of the superiority of their managerial skills. This win-lose situation can continue indefinitely as long as the managerial superiority lasts. Of course, if there is no managerial superiority, then the party ends up on the losing side of the trade transactions. Thus, one party is bound to lose.

In both comparative advantage and competitive advantage, the private and public sectors must work together to create a synergistic situation. In both of these situations, the emphasis on certain activities by both parties needs to differ. For instance, if national optimization is to be achieved through competitive advantage, then the firm is employing its managerial superiority for planning and implementing global strategies. Government in this case will make sure that nationwide human resource development through education and training is adequate to generate superior managers. On the other hand, if the country is optimizing through comparative advantage, then the firm is relying primarily on its low costs or differentiated products. Under such circumstances the government will help the company (or the industry) by trying to keep the costs stable, the national currency at a certain value level and will try to help trade relations to remain smooth along with other measures.

These measures are shown in Exhibit 9–3. The crux of the matter here is that the private sector and the government by working together can create a type of synergism that neither party can accomplish independently. But the critical point is, if the firm or industry is pursuing a comparative advantage strategy, the government should not pursue a competitive advantage strategy. Exhibit 9–2 illustrates this particular principle. If the public sector and private sector are pursuing comparative advantage simultaneously, the national economy's international trade (or international marketing) sector will be optimized. In other words, this synergism will bring about the best economic growth results through international trade. Without such synergism, the strategies that the private and public sectors use may nullify each other (Samli and Jacobs 1995).

WHAT ARE THE TOOLS?

Exhibit 9–3 illustrates different tools that are used by the public sector to support comparative advantage and competitive advantage efforts. As can be

Exhibit 9–2
Optimizing International Marketing Performance

Macro Strategies (government)

		Competitive	Comparative
Micro Strategies (Industry or Firm)	**Competitive**	National Optimization	Suboptimization
	Comparative	Suboptimization	National Optimization

Source: Samli and Jacobs (1995).

seen, the tools of these two international strategies are quite different. Comparative advantage tools would try to establish cost/price leadership as a generic strategy (Porter 1985), by having price controls or cost efficiency measures such as tax breaks, inflation controls, export stimulation measures such as grants, or trade negotiations to open up foreign markets. On the other hand, competitive advantage tools would create and implement managerial strategies that will help establish leadership in international markets. As can be seen in Exhibit 9–3, most of the tools of competitive advantage are related to infrastructure enhancement to improve international performance. Thus, the three generic strategies discussed by Porter (1985) are related to comparative advantage. Cost-price leadership, focus and differentiation are all important strategic options. However, they are micro tools related to the firm and are not as profound as the development of plans for strategic superiority that would focus on managerial expertise and proactive implementation of sophisticated strategic plans (Porter 1990). If competitive advantage becomes a macro strategy of a country such as exercised by Japan in the late 1970s and all of the 1980s, then the government must help corporate entities through the tools presented in Exhibit 9–3 (Samli and Jacobs 1995). Indeed, Japan has done very well implementing competitive advantage measures into its economy!

Perhaps the most important difference between comparative and competitive advantage is that the former emphasizes efficiency based on the key factors of production (land, labor and capital), while the latter focuses on effectiveness in education, technology and planning (managerial superiority). An international marketing strategy that would establish managerial superiority is what many authors call the multilocal orientation (Samli and Hill 1998; Wills, Samli and Jacobs 1991; Sheth and Eshagi 1989; Porter 1985).

Exhibit 9–3
Tools of the Public Sector to Support International Trade

Tools for comparative advantage	Tools for competitive advantage
Price controls	A national industrial strategy
Monetary policy for inflation control	Support for basic research
Special tax benefits for exports	Support for R &D
Cost efficiency measures	Better transportation and logistics
Government pressures to open up new markets	Cheaper energy
	Better education particularly for the labor force

This is based on developing a strategy that caters to local markets of the world according to their needs and idiosyncrasies (Samli and Jacobs 1995).

It is important to point out that both domestic and international growth strategies call for improvement in the infrastructure. Congruence in macro and micro strategies implies the macro strategy of developing the necessary infrastructure that would accommodate the micro strategies of the private sector.

ECONOMIC GROWTH IS THE ANSWER

Empowering the American consumer necessarily requires economic growth. At the point of writing this book, at least superficially, the American economy is in fine form. However, the business sector should strive to contribute more to the country's economic growth. The American economy is still not expanding as fast as possible, particularly for the lower income groups. Companies, certainly, can do more about it by ensuring their own growth. As has been said throughout this book, corporate growth can be achieved by focusing on customers, improving productivity, emphasizing new product development, enhancing service, pursuing new markets, targeting niche markets around the world, entering into strategic partnerships and training employees. Note that there are no mergers and acquisitions or downsizing in this list. As already mentioned, the federal government certainly has a major role in this economic growth process. The federal government must see to it that infrastructure development, motivating technological progress and investments, expanding international trade and improving training and education (Jasinowski 1997) are all accomplished in a satisfactory manner. In all of these areas the federal government, in addition to being a watchdog, must make contributions to energize the economy and stimulate the business sector to expand, innovate and invest.

Economic growth is a necessary condition for consumer empowerment. However this is not all by itself a sufficient condition. It is necessary but the economic performance *must be shared* with all in the society.

MUST BE FAIR TO REMAIN FREE

At this point in time, most Republicans and some Democrats do not understand the fairness doctrine. It is critical to realize that modern world history is full of revolutions and uprisings that took place because of the unfairness of the system. While the average income is just below $30,000, and chief executive officers (CEOs) and other top management members are making over $100 million a year, there is a problem regarding fairness. What is more, fairness in executive pay can be seriously questioned. If the pay of CEOs is commensurate to corporate earnings, it would be quite reasonable to justify mind-boggling salaries such as $100 million a year. But in many of the situations, if not in most, the company is not making money and may even be losing money while the CEO is getting a major increase. For instance, while in leisure-time industries the return on equity went down by 13.3 percent, executive salaries increased by 18.8 percent. The situation is more drastic for the general and special machinery industry. While between 1997 and 1998 the return on equity in that industry declined by 130.5 percent, executive pay increased by 31.75 percent.

Exhibit 9–4 illustrates different industries, percentage change in compensation to the CEOs and percentage change in the return on equity (ROE). The statistics are calculated from the means for each industry. By using Spearman's correlation technique, a correlation analysis was performed based on the total data presented in Exhibit 9–4. The calculated correlation coefficient was .32 with no significance at the 1 percent or 5 percent levels. The analysis here indicates that there is almost no connection between the firm's performance and the raises that the top management is receiving. It is rather difficult to rationalize such a system as justifiable and equitable.

Exhibit 9–4
CEO Compensation and Company Profitability

INDUSTRY	Compensation % change from 1997 (Mean for each industry)	Pay-performance % Change in ROE (Mean for each industry)
AEROSPACE	-4	58.5
APPLIANCES	529	37
BANKS & BANK HOLDING COMP	10.7	5.5
DRUGS	28.7	-42
ELECTRICAL & ELECTRONICS	-8.85	-36
GENERAL & SPECIAL MACHINERY	31.75	-130.5
BEVERAGES	5.75	22.5
BUILDING	17	-1.6
CHEMICALS	-9.8	-40
CONGLOMERATES	7.4	1.6
FOOD PROCESSING	24.4	45.4
INSTRUMENTS	9.25	-25
LEISURE-TIME INDUSTRIES	18.75	-13.3
MISCELLANEOUS MANUFACTURING	8.4	-17.6
NATURAL RESOURCES	-11	-79
NONBANK FINANCIAL	22.3	27.7
OFFICE EQUIPMENT & COMPUTERS	37.4	21.4
OIL SERVICE & SUPPLY	-27.8	-111.8
PAPER & FOREST PRODUCTS	613	788
PERSONAL CARE PRODUCTS	16	58.7
PUBLISHING, RADIO & TV BROADCAST	8.4	60.7
RAILROADS	15.3	47.3
RETAILING FOOD SERVICE	20.5	-33
RETAILING NONFOOD SERVICE	45	19.6
SERVICE INDUSTRIES	28.3	100.7
TELECOMMUNICATIONS	84.5	304.3
TEXTILES, APPAREL	-22	22.7
TOBACCO	27.2	-67
UTILITIES	28	43

Source: Calculated from data presented in *Business Week* (1999).

One fact also remains outstanding, which is that is there is no upward limit to the runaway executive pay. If this were to be contrasted to the minimum wages that are well below poverty levels, it can be concluded that we are not very careful or sensitive to outrageous inequalities. In the long run, such strong discrepancies spell nothing but trouble. This is not a new development. It has been going on for over 70 years (*Business Week*, April 19, 1999). Even though on the other end of the spectrum the lows (minimum wages) are also going up, they are not increasing at the same proportion of corporate management levels. Thus, a very large proportion of the American population is not really participating in this economic boom.

The ratio of the earning disparity between management and workers is not disappearing; it is getting worse. The French Revolution, the Russian Revolution and others were mainly caused by this disparity. One can easily argue that communism in Russia was initiated by this type of unfair situation. The critical point in this discussion is that if society is not fair, it cannot remain free. An equally important point is that the fairer the country gets by way of empowering the consumer, the wealthier all the people get, and society remains free of class warfare, revolutions and other developments such as communism or fascism that take individual freedoms away. Finally, it may be added that if the positive performance of the economy is not far-reaching, then the economic boom that is being experienced at the writing of this book is not likely to last long. The boom needs to be shared by all bar none.

SUMMARY

This chapter posits that both private and public sector's can jointly do more for the economy. Congruence between these two sectors can create a major synergism toward more desirable economic growth rates.

Government has a major responsibility to facilitate the private sector's economic growth by developing the infrastructure. By improving transportation and logistics, the energy supply, training and education, and by encouraging investments, the government can and should play a critical role.

The private sector also can focus on its customers, improve productivity, emphasize new product and service development, pursue new markets, target niche markets around the world and improve the training and education of employees. This sector can perform much better by emphasizing these focal points.

Throughout the chapter, the congruence between private and public sectors has been emphasized. Such congruence would create a major economic multiplier and achieve highly desirable economic growth, which is a necessary condition of consumer empowerment. But the society must also be fair in that all must participate in this economic growth and prosperity. This is the sufficient condition of the consumer empowerment activity. The prosperity must be shared by all and not only by a privileged few.

REFERENCES

Business Week (1999). "Executive Pay," April 19, 89–112.

Dillard, Dudley (1948). *The Economics of John Maynard Keynes*. Englewood Cliffs, NJ: Prentice Hall, Inc.

Downing, Peter, R. (1997). "Governing for Stakeholders," *Corporate Board*, 18, 13–18.

Drucker, Peter F. (1999). *Management Challenges for the 21st Century*. New York: HarperBusiness.

Friedman, M. (1970, reprinted from 1962). "The Social Responsibility of Business Is to Increase its Profits," *New York Times Magazine*, September 13.

Griffin, Jennifer J. and Mahon, John F. (1997). "The Corporate Social Performance and Corporate Financial Performance Debate: Twenty-five Years of Incomparable Research," *Business and Society*, March, 5–32.

Jasinowski, Jerry J. (1997). "The Paths to Economic Growth," *Chief Executive*, March, 48–52.

Jatusripitak, Somkid; Fahey, Liam; and Kotler, Phillip (1989). "Strategic Global Marketing: Lesson from the Japanese." In J. Sheth and A. Eshagi (eds.), *Global Marketing Perspectives*. Cincinnati: Southwestern Publishing, 125–136.

Keynes, John Maynard (1935). *The General Theory of Employment, Interest and Money*. New York, Harcourt, Brace and Company.

Lekachmon, Robert (1982). *Greed Is not Enough: Reaganomics*, New York: Pantheon Books.

Porter, Michael E. (1985). *Competitive Advantage*. New York: Free Press.

Porter, Michael E. (1990). *The Competitive Advantage of Nations*. New York: The Free Press.

Samli, A. Coskun and Hill, John S. (1998). *Marketing Globally*. Lincolnwood, IL: NTC Publishers.

Samli, A. Coskun and Jacobs, Laurence (1995). "Achieving Congruence Between Macro and Micro Generic Strategies: A Framework to Create International Competitive Advantage," *Journal of Macromarketing*, Fall, 23–32.

Sheth, Jagdish and Eshagi, Abdolreza (1989). *Global Marketing Perspectives*. Cincinnati: Southwestern Publishing.

Thomas, Cal (1999). "Bury Tax Regulations Before They Bury Us," *Jacksonville Times Union*, April 11, G-3.

Thurow, Lester (1993). *Head to Head*. New York: William Morrow.

Turban, Daniel B. and Greening, Daniel W. (1997). "Corporate Social Performance and Organizational Attractiveness to Prospective Employees." *Academy of Management Journal*, June, 658–673.

Wills, James; Samli, A. Coskun; and Jacobs, Laurence (1991). "Developing Global Products and Marketing Strategies," *Journal of Academy of Marketing Science*, Winter, 1–10.

Developing Human Resources Through Learning

A society's most important resource is manpower. The more educated people are, the more productive they become. Developing human resources has at least three distinct impacts on consumers' well-being and, commensurately, on the empowerment of consumers in our society. First, better education makes it possible for individuals to make more money and to have a better quality of life. The difference between a high school education and a college degree is approximately $600,000 in one's productive lifetime. Similarly, the difference between a college degree and a master's degree is estimated around $1 million throughout the productive life of an individual. Thus, through education, individuals make more money, and the economic base expands. Second, if they are better educated, all individuals in a society make better and more efficient decisions. This leads to overall betterment of society. Third, there are about 35 million Americans who are below the poverty line. Most of them can be rescued by better education and training. Improving the economic status of these people will contribute significantly to the enlargement of the total American market and its potential profitability.

EDUCATIONAL OBJECTIVES

As has been mentioned a few times throughout this book, human resources are the most critical asset of a society, and they must be developed and used effectively. Thus, human capital investment, which in essence is education, must be taken extremely seriously. Again, as is touched upon in different sections of this book, instead of worrying about educational excellence, domestically U.S. education is being victimized by four types of political extremism: cost, ideology, religion and profit.

Cost

Currently all of the states are driving their educational systems with cost considerations. In fact, in the early 1990s when the states' funds were rather low, some of the relatively new and less informed members of the state legislature in Florida discussed scaling down or closing down Florida universities since it was cheaper to send the young people of Florida to Georgia to get an education. The cost per pupil was much lower in Georgia at the time. This scenario did not materialize. However, the fact that it was even considered indicates the role that costs played in Florida higher education. In other words, cost has become the decisive factor in making critical decisions such as how much education, what kind of education and the like.

Almost all of the states divorce themselves from such considerations as educational excellence, educational needs of the society, educational needs of individual localities and educational needs of the citizenry of the country. State and local officials are becoming so concerned about their budgets that education is becoming a *social privilege* rather then a *social right*. In other words, those who can afford it are likely to get a good education. And those who cannot afford it are likely to start work life in a handicapped situation— uninformed and unskilled. College tuition since the early 1980s has been going up much faster than inflation or increases in income.

Perhaps the most important aspect of this cost-driven education is what is called "distance learning." Instead of seeking qualified faculties and encouraging them to be engaged in classroom learning through interactive give and take, universities are embarking upon information technology to offer courses and degrees. These virtual classrooms and virtual universities are threatening legitimate and well-established programs. This, again, is an indication of the cost-driven nature of our education system. As opposed to small class sizes, interactive communication, opportunity for individuals to exercise their creativity and be guided by their mentors, the educational process is shifted to computers. The problem with distance learning is that it is not clear how much learning is taking place. Distant dissemination of information is not distance learning. Furthermore, learning through computer (using only one of the five senses, vision) is likely not as effective as using all five senses as is done in a classroom. Additionally, one might ask, could a computer screen motivate a student as a master teacher would in a classroom?

Ideology

Some people in our society have a very antagonistic approach toward anything that is public. They do not like government and they think everything, perhaps with the exception of the armed forces, needs to be privatized. Thus they are trying very hard to destroy the public education system that is so essential for American society. Without a proper public education system, it is impossible to create and maintain a middle class in our society or in any society. The middle class is the backbone of the American society. It is the stabilizing factor for our society. Most societies, particularly those located south of the border, that do not have an adequately large and growing middle class, are plagued by political unrest and revolutions. If there were no public education, those who could afford schooling would pay large sums for private education, and those who could not afford it would remain uneducated. The middle class would slowly disappear. The gap between the rich and poor would enlarge, and society would become much more unstable because of the ensuing political unrest.

One additional aspect of ideology is related to statism. As discussed earlier, some people think that the federal government cannot do nearly as good a job in educating the people as can individual states. In a different context, statism versus federalism is discussed in chapter 6. Suffice it to say that if each state does something different for education by maintaining significantly different standards, it becomes very difficult to establish national standards. Without these standards, it is impossible to maintain a competitive position in the global marketplace. Nor is it possible for consumers to be mobile or flexible enough to change jobs and improve themselves. It has been said that the Japanese, German and French systems of education are the best in the world and they all are very heavily centralized programs.

Religion

Religious zealots in American society always have been against public education where state and religion are separated. Although it has no impact on the quality of education, school prayers have been an issue for a long time. Anti-public-education sentiment, thus, is generated through religion and spills over to other aspects of public education beyond school prayers and Bible studies. It has infiltrated into curriculum development, research and many other aspects of education. It is more than dangerous to impose biblical (or other religious) values that are over two thousand years old upon cyber-age educational needs.

Only one society in modern times tried such an experiment, and today Iran is at least half a century behind the industrialized world. It tried to apply Islamic laws to a country that was desperately in need of industrial development. According to this author, any type of zealotry can create a tremendous hurdle to educational advancement that would have the answers to the constantly increasing complexities of society, and that would enhance its survival and accelerate its progress. Religious values, time and again, interfere with most recent research trends. Fetal tissue research, cloning and other extremely promising research thrusts have come under very serious criticism from the religious community.

Profit

At this time many for-profit private schools are entering into the American educational pastures. Many of these simply do not have enough experiences, qualifications and strong motivation to teach. Their best courses, their most creative programs will disappear very quickly if they are not yielding profit. This is a very dangerous and negative trend in the American human resource development.

It must be reiterated that the four key barriers of cost, ideology, religion and profit must be overcome because, more and more, individuals' positions in our society will be determined by their knowledge. Unless individuals have good educational backgrounds, they will not advance, get better jobs and make contributions to society's well-being. Our society, therefore, will have to invest in intelligence based on education and learning so that individuals can develop their own personal educational profiles. In other words, American society must go beyond all the hurdles to become a *learning society* ("European Commission White Paper" 1997).

GROWTH IN THE MARKETPLACE

In order for the American economy to grow at a sustainable and satisfactory rate, the empowerment of the American consumer is a necessary condition. However, this empowerment must take place within the constraints of American society as a *learning society*. In other words, America as a whole must take education very seriously and strive for the highest possible levels of education.

At least three key driving forces are behind the change and growth at this time that necessitate the emergence of a learning society: information, globalization and science and technology. The "European Commission White Paper" (1997) analyzes these three forces, which are as important in the United States as they are in Europe.

First, the information society is transforming the nature of work and the organization of production. It is forcing everyone in these organizations to adapt, first, to new technical tools and, second, to dramatic changes in working conditions.

Second, globalization is changing the job-creation process in society in a dramatic fashion. It is blurring the dividing lines among job markets. Additionally, it is forcing management to raise the general level of qualification of workers and employees. This demands still further improvements in existing skills or totally new skills on the part of production workers.

Third, science and technology are being developed at an increasing rate. Furthermore, they are more and more applied to production methods. These technologies must be fully utilized by the industrial sectors of the economy so that the whole society could benefit from the optimal usage of these technologies.

The education-driven learning society must perform at least five key functions in order to cope with the three key driving forces as identified above ("European Commission White Paper" 1997):

1. Encourage people to broaden their knowledge level. It must make information available for all so that knowledge levels can be broadened.

2. Strengthen links between schools and companies by developing opportunities for people to work and receive practical experience while they are in school. In fact, the link between schools and work may become a life-long learning proposition.

3. Create second opportunities through schools so that people, regardless of age or geographic location, will not be shut out from the school system. High-quality educational resources would help some people who otherwise would have been left out of the education system and subsequently would have suffered social exclusion.

4. Develop better knowledge of languages and other cultures. Language is a major asset that enables people to interact more easily with other people, to discover other cultures and values and to stimulate an individual's intellectual agility. Understanding other cultures expands an individual's perception of life and facilitates greater capability for decision-making.

5. Invest in training and education. Whereas capital investments are rather carefully planned, in equipment and production systems, investment in training of personnel in the corporate entity is woefully neglected. However, balancing these two would significantly stimulate market growth. In other words, investment in capital and investment in human resources should be equalized. Furthermore, it is necessary to take advantage of ever-increasing technological sophistication, by proportionately increasing skills to use the technology properly. Advanced education would accomplish that.

These five key functions must and would lead in the direction of human conditioning in a society that is determined to become a learning society. Individuals in such a society will display (of course to a varying degree and in different forms) five powerful tendencies that would distinguish a *learning society* from others. The first four tendencies are articulated by Thurow (1999) and the fifth one is mine which basically summarizes the first four. The five tendencies are (1) curiosity, (2) exploration, (3) learning, (4) building and (5) improving. These are briefly discussed below.

Being Curious: Wondering why things work the way they do is not an automatic or natural characteristic. During the Dark Ages, for instance, people had forgotten such basic knowledge as how to fertilize agricultural fields. As knowledge declined, standards of living also fell. During that era there was no belief in learning and progress (Thurow 1999). If people take things as given and do not develop a curiosity as to how to improve their surroundings, obviously there cannot be any progress in that society.

Wanting to Explore: Being curious and putting this curiosity to work are simply two different activities. Exploring the unknown by having the courage to go where no one has gone before is essential for progress. Anything from space explorations to the development of the Internet in our day and age reflect such an orientation.

Willing to Learn: Having an open mind and thirst for new knowledge are not givens. Human beings need to be conditioned for such behaviors. A learning society cannot evolve if the people are not willing to learn. The desire to push for knowledge is a human condition that is the essence of progress.

Wishing to Build: One of the key characteristics of American society is learning through doing. Accumulating practical knowledge is critical for a tendency to build to be present. There is active and passive learning. Active learning is through individual endeavor and experiences and passive learning is learning from others' experiences. Both are important; however, it may be argued that active learning is more likely to lead to wishing to build. Putting all the learning into application provides a special dynamism to the society.

Ambition to Improve: Finally, in some cultures there is a fatalistic attitude such as "what is" definitely is what it was predestined and will remain that way. Getting out of such a fatalistic mode and instilling in its people the ambition to improve and never stop is what a society must aim at if it wants to become a thriving learning society. Exhibit 10–1 illustrates the essentials of a learning society that is a prerequisite for empowering the consumer. The learning society improves the decision-making process in all walks of society. Therefore it is essential.

Information, globalization, and science and technology will particularly help markets grow if education and training activities are commensurate with the varying developments in these dramatic sources of economic power. But the education part must be paid particular attention. Otherwise, these dramatic sources of economic power will not function well, and society will further be divided into upper class and under class.

EDUCATION AND THE INDIVIDUAL DECISION PROCESS

In 1992 it was written that America has been in a panic about education for at least a decade. A major problem in the American education system has been a group of dropouts and poorly educated students that are virtually unemployable ("The Drop-out Society" 1992). In 1981 it was estimated that 23 million American adults were functionally illiterate. This situation did not improve during the Reagan and Bush eras (DePaolo 1993). The factors (cost, ideology and profit) that are discussed earlier are fighting off the attempts of the Clinton administration to improve the conditions. As they fight off the attempts to improve the public education system, they also blame the public education system for all the ills of our younger generation: drugs, crimes, lack of ambition and the like.

Perhaps the importance of education can be illustrated with the findings of an earlier study. In 1994 *American Demographics* reported that over 40 percent of the people with the lowest literacy skills are poor. However, only

Exhibit 10–1
Excelling in Decision-Making

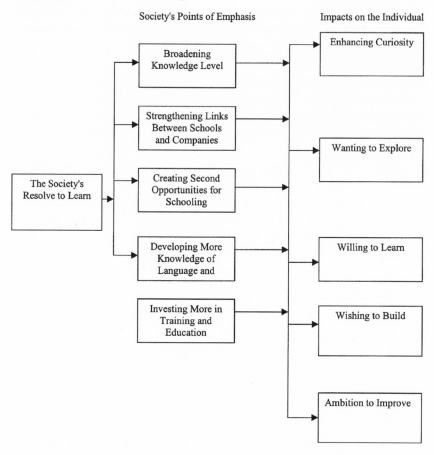

10 percent of the people with the highest literacy skills are still poor, indicating that education can uplift the economic status in a very significant way.

With better education, not only do consumers have a better chance to get
a good job but they are also likely to perform better in those jobs (Robinson
and Schroeder, 1993). This is so because education leads in the direction of
enabling individuals to make better decisions and implement their knowledge in complex problems that they encounter.

If educated individuals can make better decisions, raising the educational
level of the American populace, by definition, would imply better decision-
making for the individual in all aspects of life. Cumulatively, if all individuals
are making good decisions about, say, health, personal care, individual de-

velopment and consumption patterns, then better decisions will also be made for society as a whole. The corporate world has been cognizant of this fact for a long time. Not only do corporations pay the expenses for their executives to go to school, they also offer executive education programs as part of their efforts to keep up with the ever-changing and sometimes even turbulent business environment. Factors such as business globalization, technological innovations and strategic alliances have expanded the number of business universities from 400 in 1987 to over 1,000 in 1997 (Greco 1997). However, the same privileges are not quite available to nonexecutive personnel. In other words, the average worker often does not have access to these business universities that are directly associated with and run by corporate entities. The corporate entity simply does not put enough into its workers' education or training. Thus the corporate world is depriving itself and the total American society by not attempting to train all of its people better.

CORPORATE DECISION-MAKING AND LEARNING

Some years ago, in dealing with the switch from being an industrial society to an information society, Naisbitt (1982, p. 37) stated that "we are moving from the specialist who is soon obsolete to the generalist who can adapt." Drucker (1992) commented that the quickest way for a person living in a developed society to make a decent living was to become a semiskilled machine operator. But that is over. Today the same person can make a middle-class living only through learning and accumulating knowledge.

Some corporations have been practicing training, knowing full well that if their employees are well trained, they will perform better. These training programs may not be sufficiently long or adequate enough, but they clearly indicate higher levels of effectiveness (Shepherd and Ridnour 1996). Unfortunately, not all corporations are sharing such views and such activities.

The importance of learning in organizations has become greater as individuals in the organization share new understandings of the nature of their organization and their changing world to generate new behavior (Waldersee 1997). In other words, organizational learning must be passed onto individuals who are attached to that organization.

Organizations must learn to survive and to succeed. Learning takes place in organizations as long as they survive, but this organizational learning must be converted into the creation of learning organizations. In an organization, learning takes place in an unsystematic manner. In such cases, the information that is being obtained is not necessarily shared or utilized by the organization unless it becomes a *learning organization*. Becoming a learning organization implies a conscious effort of imparting these learned experiences and derived knowledge to be shared with those who work there, so that knowledge will be available in the right places at the right times as it is needed. Unlike organizational learning, in learning organizations knowledge is institutionalized, strategically placed and used as needed. Thus there is a major difference between organizational learning and the learning organization. The latter systematically and proactively uses knowledge in its dealings with its workers to enhance the company's competitive advantage. In this day and age of information, creating organizational information proactively is almost a necessity for those who want to survive and excel in the marketplace.

There are many different ways of becoming a learning organization. In essence, information and experience do not accumulate proportionately throughout an organization. Furthermore, all information and experiences are not of equal importance for the organization. Thus, to become a learning organization, there must be a certain type of leadership to generate and locate within the organization ever-changing information and experiences. Thus there will be a continuity between the changing needs and information and the experience base of a firm. But because of the changes in the marketplace and varied experiences, information generated and skills developed often stay and accumulate in different parts of the organization and are not always available where and when they are really needed. As a major prerequisite for learning organizations, an intellectual transformation of the workforce is necessary (Waldersee 1997). In such cases, management uses its interactions with employees and webs of information sources to create a higher intellectual atmosphere that will make employees more adaptable and more effective in dealing with changes and new functions. Furthermore, Fulmer, Gibbs, and Keys (1998) maintain that at least four categories of learning tools are needed by learning organizations: (1) maintenance tools to implement existing strategies, (2) anticipating tools to create future strategies, (3) crossover tools to switch from current to future ways of thinking and (4) utility tools used for all types of strategy development. Needless to say, these tools must be used effectively and with caution in order for the learning organization to generate and implement adequate knowledge.

Corresponding to both organizational learning and learning organizations, in recent years a new unit in the organization has emerged that houses information (or knowledge) workers (Drucker 1999). If that unit generates proper and necessary information and makes it available for the whole organization, then the whole corporate structure has a chance to be more effective.

Just as organizations need to learn to become learning organizations and create a division of information workers, society must also have similar objectives. In developing human resources in the marketplace, society must try to give students the capacity and the knowledge to continue learning and, above all, the desire to do so (Drucker 1999). Thus developing human resources is related to two essential factors, *education* and *training*. All consumers in the marketplace must have access to both. As I tried to illustrate by giving some corporate examples, society will be better off by providing better education to all. Knowledge is power; therefore, empowering the consumer leads to better education and training for individuals so that powerful human resources can be created and maintained.

DECISION-MAKING AND COMPETITIVE ADVANTAGE

Porter (1985) talks about competitive advantage that is based on strategic superiority which, in turn, implies better decision-making capabilities. Thus far in this chapter, we have maintained that, both in the corporate entity and within society, better education leads to learning, which is the crucial way to improve human resources.

At the corporate level, companies that are learning organizations are more capable of forecasting changes and faster to react to changes occurring in the marketplace. They are able to adjust easily and to be much more flexible than other firms. Learning organizations are much more alert for potential problems and trouble. These organizations create new knowledge and encourage their employees to expand their own knowledge base by sharing the knowledge created by the organization. In other words, the entire organization has the capability of learning as an entire body (Redding 1997).

What is described for the learning organizations above is applicable to what I have termed the *learning society*. In a market economy, all decisions made by the government, by the corporate entity and by the consumer count. It must be so that all these decision-makers can make better decisions. This would improve society's overall well-being, its utilization of resources and its efficiencies in production as well as in distribution. Thus, the accumulation of human capital (or societal learning) is very critical in productivity growth. But it is equally critical in creating income inequality. Just minor differences in individual talents, preferences and economic support they receive can create serious income inequalities (Benabou 1996). If a society is

Exhibit 10–2
Excelling in Decision-Making

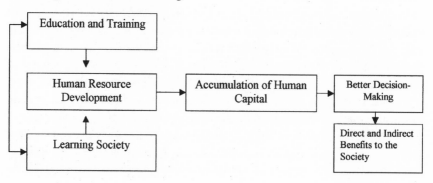

a learning society, it has to make the fruits of this learning available to all and not to the privileged few.

Perhaps a major question should be raised here: can a society excel in decision-making? This is one of the key premises of a democratic society which has a market economy that has not been carefully articulated. Instead dogmas such as "Leave it to free market to solve all the problems," or "Take the government out of the picture and everything will be just fine" dominate our society's affairs and, unfortunately, perhaps its destiny. This author believes that a society could excel in decision-making itself; however, without having access to effective education and the knowledge base, all consumers will not be benefiting from the ability and opportunity to make personal economic decisions. If consumers do not have access to the knowledge to make better decisions, society as a whole cannot materialize its full economic potential. Thus everyone loses.

Based on our discussion in this chapter, Exhibit 10–2 is constructed. The underlying factor in the exhibit is the presence of a learning society. If society overall is not making a genuine effort to generate and disseminate information, the whole picture becomes an exercise in futility. Society must be involved in learning that is not driven by cost, ideology and religion. With this basic premise, by using education and training activities more effectively, we can create a learning society and develop human resources more adequately. Development of human resources leads in the direction of human capital accumulation, which is equally (if not more) as important as financial capital for society's well-being. Herein lies the connection between human resource development and human capital. They lead to better decision-making that is critical in empowering consumers. If consumers can

make better decisions, everybody wins because there will be a social optimization of decisions in the direction of advancing both the individual and
society simultaneously. Society cannot stand still; it must reach out and develop further. This cannot happen unless its human resources are developed.
Exhibit 10–2 establishes the necessary pattern for human resource development in the United States that is a prerequisite for the empowerment of
all consumers.

A learning-oriented society develops excellent educational and training
opportunities, which directly improve the earning capacity of consumers and
accelerate development of human capital. Indirectly, better education improves everyone's capability to make good economic decisions. This also has
a significant impact in the well-being of the national economy. One must
also explore just what happens if society does not become a learning society.
One may explore the impact of the Industrial Revolution. The development
of the steam engine gave rise to the Industrial Revolution. Factories
emerged, mass production became a reality, but social consequences went
far beyond efficiency in productivity. According to some historians, the ex-
plosive growth of the steam-engine-based textile industry revived slavery
(Drucker 1999), because there was a huge demand for low-cost labor. The
factory took worker and work out of the home and started the early warnings
of the "family crisis" that is experienced in modern industrial societies. One
may question the uses of cyberspace and information technology. If the
booming information technology cannot be shared with all consumers and
if very large masses are left behind in participating and sharing the benefits
of the information technology explosion, slavery of a different sort can be
revived again just as it was at the beginning of the Industrial Revolution.
Here once again, human resource development activities must be put in the
forefront of societal priorities so that large masses will not be left behind in
benefiting from the on-going revolution.

SUMMARY

This chapter posits that society's human resources must be developed, and
it equates human resource development activity with education. Education
must be quality-driven rather than driven by cost, ideology, religion or
profit. It must be connected to what this author calls the learning society.
The idea of a learning society stems from learning organizations. Organizations that are progressive and that excel in the marketplace are organized
around being learning organizations. The same concept can be applied to
society as a whole. Society is facing challenges particularly from three key

developments: information, globalization and science and technology. Our society will be better off as a learning society to cope with these most powerful developments. In order for our society to become a learning society, it must perform at least five key functions: (1) broaden the knowledge level, (2) strengthen links between schools and companies, (3) create second opportunities through schools, (4) develop better knowledge of languages and (5) invest in training and education. The human resources of our society are bound to develop between education in schools and training on the job. This development has both direct and indirect impacts on consumer empowerment in our society. Developed human resources in a learning society will have the tendency for enhancing curiosity, wanting to explore, willing to learn, wishing to build and ambition to improve.

Another key point posited by this chapter is that the individual decision-making process improves with better education. Even if this were to be the only benefit that development of human resources could yield, this would be quite worthwhile. If all of the people in our society make better decisions in their daily lives, natural resources will be better used, society's efficiency will go up and the overall quality of life will be improved.

REFERENCES

American Demographics (1994). "The Lowdown on Literacy," June, 6–7.

"European Commission White Paper on Education and Training Arguments for a Learning Society" (1997). *Journal of European Industrial Training*, February–March, 1.

"The Drop-out Society?" (1992). *The Economist*, November 21, S7–10.

Benabou, Roland (1996). "Equity and Efficiency in Human Capital Investment—the Local Connection," *Review of Economic Studies*, April, 237–265.

De Paolo, Ron (1993). "A Nation at Risk—Still," *Across the Board*, March, 16–24.

Drucker, Peter F. (1999). "Beyond the Information Revolution," *The Atlantic Monthly*, October, 47–57.

Drucker, Peter F. (1992). *Managing for the Future*. New York: Truman Talley Books.

Fulmer, Robert M., Gibbs, Philip, and Keys, J. Bernard (1998). "The Second Generation Learning Organizations: New Tools for Sustaining Competitive Advantage," *Organizational Dynamics*, Autumn, 7–19.

Greco, JoAnn (1997). "Corporate Schooling," *Journal of Business Strategy*, May–June, 48–53.

Naisbitt, John (1982). *Megatrends*. New York: Warner Books.

Porter, Michael E. (1985). *Competitive Advantage*. New York: The Free
    Press.
Redding, John (1997). *Training and Development*, No. 8, 61–68.
Robinson, Alan G. and Schroeder, Dean M. (1993). "Training Continuous
    Improvement and Human Relations," *California Management Review*,
    Winter, 35–58.
Shepherd, David C. and Ridnour, Rick E. (1996). "A Comparison of the
    Sales Management Training Practices of Smaller and Larger Orga-
    nizations," *Journal of Business and Industrial Marketing*, No. 2, 37–47.
Thurow, Lester C. (1999). *Building Wealth*. New York: HarperCollins.
Waldersee, Robert (1997). "Becoming a Learning Organization—the Trans-
    formation of the Workforce," *Journal of Management Development*,
    No. 4, 262–274.

Chapter 11

The Environment Infrastructure and Consumer Empowerment

We are told daily that the gross domestic product in America is up, our economy is moving forward and we are all doing well. But we also know that Americans are working longer and harder just to keep up with the enormous cost of social and environmental breakdown. Although thus far in this book we have touched upon both social and environmental issues, we have spent more time discussing social breakdown in terms of the accumulation of economic power through merger mania, inequality in the distribution of income and excessive powers of the medical, financial, legal and technological sectors. It must also be understood that there is a tremendous cost of environmental breakdown that is due to misuse of resources as well as neglect of the infrastructure. When consumer empowerment is being considered, it is critical to examine the impact of a deteriorating environment or a changing GDP in terms of its quality on consumers, knowing full well that these are totally out of consumers' power and control.

In calculating the GDP almost everything Americans spend indiscriminately is added up as total goods. But if hundreds of billions of dollars that are spent to cope with crime, lawyers, excessive medical costs and cost accruing from environmental deterioration are all increasing improportionately and taking a big chunk of the GDP, then the quality of the GDP is going down. All these costs are included in that total goods (Baker 1999). Unless we can show genuine progress in the GDP, there is truly a big question regarding its quality. This is a topic that is not even acknowledged by economic and government sectors, let alone by political parties. Therefore it is not at all discussed in attempts to evaluate the American economy's performance.

In this chapter, we will explore some of the basic conditions that are related to the quality of GDP through infrastructure maintenance and improvement. In order to achieve an increased quality of GDP, it is critical to realize that there should be a central guiding force such as the federal government that has the proper orientation toward the well-being of not only special interest groups, but all consumers. Perhaps one of the most important reasons for having such a central guiding force is that human beings are all short-run-oriented and, much of the time, are not quite disciplined in terms of planning for the future. As a result, they find it difficult to save for a "rainy day." When there is a choice, for instance, between medical saving vouchers and medical insurance, they are more likely to spend the voucher-driven savings today and not to have medical insurance tomorrow. When it comes to consumer spending, people are not known for their concern about the environment and will not put away money, in terms of savings, to take care of and maintain the environment via developing the infrastructure. Furthermore, those consumers who are concerned about these issues are virtually powerless. They cannot individually make adjustments or take certain steps in their lifestyles that would make enough of a difference on environmental or infrastructural issues.

On the other end of the spectrum, the private business sector, which has much to say about environmental and infrastructural issues, typically opts for short-run profit at the expense of the environment and the infrastructure. Thus, if anything, society must have a central authority that would perform certain duties that individuals (and businesses) could not, would not and perhaps even should not perform. The government, elected properly and empowered correctly, can perform these functions. Among these functions are developing and maintaining the infrastructure within which the economy survives and thrives, maintaining an environment that is pollution free or creating the conditions for a free as well as fair trade both at home and abroad. The economic development within the country must be sustainable. But as stated in an editorial in *Business Week* (Jan. 17, 2000), economic growth cannot be and should not be taken for granted. Certain government policies are needed to maintain current prosperity.

IMPROVING THE LINKAGE BETWEEN THE ECONOMY AND THE INFRASTRUCTURE

A national sustainable development action strategy is likely to foster the economic vitality of the United States (Charnovitz 1996). Thus, sustainable economic development policy that should be a nonpolitical issue is a critical goal. Improving the linkage between the economy and the infrastructure is essential for this economic sustainability.

In order to achieve sustainable development, it must be understood that the pursuit of one set of goals affects others and, therefore, we must develop and implement policies that integrate economic, environmental and social goals simultaneously.

Similarly, there should be environmental regulations that are reasonable to comply with and, therefore, the industry can almost voluntarily implement them rather than fighting them every inch of the way. One of the key problems in achieving sustainable development is related to the use of public resources. The commercial beneficiaries of these resources, including land, air and water, need to be charged the full cost of their depletion or use of these resources (Charnovitz 1996). Drucker (1999) maintains that many companies are returning less to the economy than what they use up in resources or might add what they create in terms of pollution in the economy. This situation does not lead to a sustainable development strategy. Such a strategy above all must positively link the economy to the environment.

Perhaps the best way to improve the linkage between the economy and the environment is establishing an environmental friendliness measure of all products that are produced.

ASSESSING ENVIRONMENT FRIENDLINESS

Waterways served as industrial pollution sites; skies dispersed smoke from factories and power plants and the land proved to be a cheap and convenient place to dump industrial and urban wastes. (Samli 1998).

This situation has not improved substantially. In fact, our current levels of resource consumption and waste generation are not considered sustainable in the long run (Sarkis and Rasheed 1995). In a more dramatic manner, Hart (1997, 67) describes the situation as "depleted farmland, fisheries and forests, choking urban pollution; poverty; infectious disease; and migration are spilling over geopolitical borders." He further posits that as we try to satisfy our needs, we are destroying the ability of future generations to do the same. In other words, the quality of GDP is deteriorating, and future generations will have a much more difficult time satisfying their needs.

The environmental deterioration is caused by many products varying from spray cans to cholorofluorocarbons (CFCs) to nuclear energy that is generating uncontrollable nuclear waste. While CFCs are causing significant genetic changes or contributing to skin cancer by creating holes in the ozone layer, nuclear and other toxic wastes are causing a very substantial increase in birth defects and various forms of cancer (Mahon and Kelley 1987).

It has been estimated that toxic air pollution has added up to 2.7 billion pounds of pollutants a year (Easterbrook 1989). The water we drink has constantly increasing levels of carcinogens; foods we consume have DDT residue and other carcinogens. All heavy industries generate hazardous waste. As these industries dispose of waste, they create superfund sites. There are some 2,000 dangerous chemical dumping places throughout the country, the cleaning of which will, at least, cost about $21 million per site (Office of Solid Waste Emergency Response 1988).

Underground gasoline storage tanks are creating another major problem. Approximately 80 percent of these are constructed of unprotected steel. Thus they are likely to rust and allow gasoline to seep through and pollute the land and groundwater (Samli 1998). The cleanup process will cost at least $1 million per spill. In addition to very serious health hazard considerations, the cleanup process is an extreme cost burden to the society. Spending large sums on such activities will make it more difficult for society to improve its economic well-being (Samli 1998). Thus, even if we succeed in empowering consumers in our society, they will still be receivers of a deteriorating GDP in terms of quality, partly due to deteriorating environmental conditions and neglected infrastructure.

As a matter of fact, the deteriorating environment and the infrastructure are very closely related. Indeed, if the infrastructure is not taken care of, there will be further acceleration in environmental deterioration.

At least three key areas of environmental deterioration can be singled out: production of dangerous chemicals and industrial waste, underground spills of storage tanks, and overuse and depletion of scarce resources (Samli 1998).

These and many other possible environmental deterioration possibilities must be dealt with if economic sustainability is to be achieved. Unfortunately, thus far in the United States, our method has been to try to find a solution as the problem approaches extremely dangerous proportions. The Environmental Protection Agency and superfunds are simple indications of this approach. They came into being when conditions got critically dangerous. It is important to realize that a reactive approach to such problems is not good enough. First, by the time society reacts, it is rather too late and much damage has been done. Second, cleaning up a mess after it caused a lot of damage is much more expensive than preventing it before it happens.

The problem stems from the fact that a concept such as "social cost" has not been taken seriously. All products, as they are produced, create both a social cost and a private cost. Although we have developed extremely sophisticated cost accounting techniques to determine the private cost, we have not been very enterprising in exploring the public cost (Samli 1998). Public cost would be a measure to determine the environmental friendliness of a proposed new product. If it is environmentally unfriendly, then this would be factored into the equation before the product is produced and later when it is priced. Having such a social cost calculation as a factor in costing out a prospective product is likely to create a greater in-depth analysis of generating more environmental friendly products or even abandoning some before they are produced.

RECONCILING ECONOMIC AND ECOLOGICAL FACTORS

A few years ago, Sheth and Parvatiyar (1995) coined the term "sustainable marketing" that analyzed how economic and environmental factors can be reconciled. They maintained that it can be accomplished by reinventing products and product systems. Such reinvention must satisfy two principles of physics. First, the principle of conservation of mass means the total quantity of input resource materials must be equal to output. Output here includes the sum of usable products, waste, emissions and other releases. Second, the principle of waste deals with the energy being "banked" or "embedded" into the finished products (Fuller 1999). In other words, what goes in comes out, either as a product or a waste component. However, two points are very critical. First, in the conversion process of inputs to outputs, the lesser waste indicates a greater environmental responsibility. This depends upon the company's environmental philosophy as well as its production efficiency. Second, the efficient conversion process is very dependent on the infrastructure in that the firm cannot be quite efficient in its activities unless there is an adequate and constantly improving infrastructure.

At least in part, it is the infrastructure that enables the reconciliation of economic and ecological factors. As the infrastructure is developed or modernized, many of the measures that are taken would have major environmental implications. For instance, as new energy sources are developed they can be made more environment friendly, or when the national transportation facilities are examined they can be improved in the most environment friendly manner. It must be reiterated that the consumer is not powerful enough to exert any power or control on either ecological or infrastructure-related issues.

In some ways the infrastructure is the moderator of the relationship between the environment and the consumer. If a business wants to be environmentally responsible—that is, zero waste and zero discharge (Fuller 1999)—then it must be functioning within the constraints of a substantially improved infrastructure.

IMPROVING THE INFRASTRUCTURE

If we accept that the role of modern corporations is to provide conditions under which economic opportunities for individuals may flourish, then we must examine the infrastructure (Danley 1995). Unlike some others, this author maintains that there is a significant relationship between infrastructure expenditures and industrial productivity. Exhibit 11–1 reflects the author's calculations expressed in terms of percent change. It is further assumed that there is a lead-lag relationship between the two. Indeed a three-year lead-lag relationship indicates that there is a high correlation between infrastructure development expenditures and the increase in productivity that materializes. Three years later, calculations yielded a person's correlation coefficient of .56. In this analysis, productivity included total shipments divided by total number of employees. Infrastructure figures are based on total direct expenditure on infrastructure-related activities. It is important to realize that unless careful planning goes into infrastructure development and unless it is understood that the expected results will not materialize fully in less than three or four years, not much can be expected. Despite other studies indicating a strong link between the infrastructure and economic growth (Robles 1998), there is no relief in sight. The existing infrastructure is not carefully examined, and there are no plans devoted to or funds allocated to rebuilding it. Nor are there any plans to improve it further. This improvement is necessary for the advanced technologies of today.

Because the infrastructure has a very strong role in the private sector's productivity as well as the environmental well-being of society, it is essential that much attention be paid to its improvement. Empowering the consumer in both of these issues is totally up to the government and the business sector.

Many of the improvements in the infrastructure do not necessarily appear directly in private productivity. But there is no doubt about the fact that

Exhibit 11-1
Direct Expenditures in Infrastructure and Growth in Productivity, 1985-95

	Direct Expenditures (millions of $)	Variation of Direct Expenditures	Productivity ($)	Variation in Productivity in %
1985	$656,188.00		$21,782.55	-2.15
1986	$715,324.00	9	$21,314.45	3.31
1987	$772,863.00	8	$22,020.63	6.45
1988	$824,507.00	6.7	$23,441.31	3.25
1989	$890,000.00	7.9	$24,202.76	2.04
1990	$972,662.00	9.3	$24,695.96	-1.9
1991	$1,059,805.00	8.9	$24,227.02	5.37
1992	$1,146,610.00	8.2	$25,527.11	3.41
1993	$1,210,096.00	5.5	$26,398.41	5.46
1994	$1,260,642.00	4.2	$27,839.91	4.76
1995	$1,347,763.00	6.9	$29,164.64	2.54

Source: Statistical Abstract of the United States, various issues.

infrastructure improvement reduces inefficiencies in the private sector. These improvements can be in the form of energy, communication, roads and warehouses, education and others. All of these directly or indirectly influence the ecology.

DEVELOPING ENERGY

One of the most important aspects of industrial productivity is developing cheap and plentiful energy. However, energy development, as discussed earlier in this chapter, can create environmental adversities. Some energy sources such as coal, nuclear means or other fossil fuels are all environmentally offensive and cause serious pollution.

At the writing of this book, alternative energy sources are not seriously explored. Whereas during the times of President Nixon, energy independence programs were initiated emphasizing synthetic fuels, all of these programs were discontinued during President Reagan's era. While most of the motor vehicles in Brazil are run by alcohol, in the United States the petroleum lobby has sued the American government and won the case against maintaining 15 percent or so ethanol in petroleum for automobiles. Again, whereas American know-how can convert even garbage into energy, such initiatives are blocked by big energy-generating oligopolies.

But what happens when the fossil fuel supplies dry out? What happens when the nuclear waste that is a threat to life on this earth reaches critical levels and cannot be stored any longer? Developing low-cost, safe and plentiful energy is a major challenge in modern industrial society, and certainly the government must play a role in it, since private interests are not acting responsibly regarding the environment and the future.

COMMUNICATION SYSTEMS

If information does not flow in society, the private sector cannot be productive. There will be no information about markets, availability of raw materials, semifinished goods and sourcing opportunities, nor will products be where they should be when they should be. The essence of productivity is highly dependent on having an adequate communication system. With new developments in cyberspace, cable TV, cell phones and other communication devices, the picture is rather muddied. It is critical that the citizenry have access to and participate in the communication process that keeps our society together. Thus, the communication system must be all-inclusive. Again, the government plays a very critical role in the development of such a system. Much of the computer and telephone communication nets are based on the U.S. government's original investments in fiber optics and other infrastructure developments.

ROADS AND OTHER SUPPORT SYSTEMS

The flow of finished goods, raw materials and semifinished products is extremely critical for society's productivity. Particularly the movement of the necessary materials has become more and more critical as just-in-time (JIT) systems have been put to use.

Effective functioning of JIT systems is also dependent upon the availability of proper warehousing systems. If the backup parts, components or raw materials are not available when needed, the total process of moving the finished products to the point of purchase for consumers' convenience will be hindered.

Poor transportation systems not only reduce the private sector's productivity but also can cause many serious accidents that further harm consumers' well-being. Many trucks or trains carrying environmentally sensitive materials have accidents throughout the year. Such mishaps are not quite factored into the equation regarding the infrastructure, industrial activity and consumer well-being. However, they need to be stopped. Better roads and driving regulations are critical in this area.

ECONOMY MUST BE STRONG NOT TO LOSE FACTORIES

Both the environment and the infrastructure lead in the direction of attracting and/or discouraging manufacturing and other high-tech producers. There is a very sensitive balance between suitability of the environment and stringency of regulations. On one hand, companies would like to have a powerful and up-to-date total infrastructure; however, they certainly don't like paying taxes. This contradiction makes it difficult for the federal government to keep the environment and the infrastructure up to date. In the meantime, if the environment and the infrastructure are not adequate, companies move out of the country (Bleakley 1995). This last option is not at all good for American consumers. If companies move to Mexico, they will take well-paying jobs with them and leave hamburger-flipping types of jobs behind (see chapter 2). Thus the economy must be very strong regarding the infrastructure so that not only on-going companies will be encouraged to stay in the country but also new manufacturing establishments will enter the market and be successful. The strength of the economy is, at least partially, dependent on having an industrial policy for the country as a whole that would optimize the American economic performance and provide some general direction for the market system. Within this industrial policy there must be provisions for international trade to be free as well as fair.

FREE AND FAIR TRADE

Trade, both domestic and international, is not fair by definition as it is made free, as very aptly articulated by Danley (1995). Corporations strive for doing business with the least amount of hindrance with their ability to transfer assets, production and capital across the borders. In this relentless pursuit of profits, low costs and strategic advantages, corporations appear to be superseding both society's and the nation's best interests.

This is a grim observation in the sense that the interest of the company should never supersede the national interest. However, the scenario is rather plausible. This is one of the reasons why governments and corporate entities must work cooperatively in partnerships and why they should not function in old-fashioned adversarial relationships.

The scenario presented above is not totally American. Japanese electronics makers have relocated their production in different parts of Asia. They are still seeking lower cost production possibilities by using more local parts and by seeking cheaper production sites (Ishibahsi 1996). In such cases, the question remains the same: Are company and national benefits likely to be the same, and is a company's moving freely in the international arena likely to benefit consumers indiscriminately. In order for such a situation to materialize, first there must be free trade. Hindrances to trade are likely to deny benefit to consumers everywhere.

However, free trade advocates forget the second condition here: Is there fair trade? The fairness of trade has a number of requirements. First, the proceeds of trade should be shared fairly. If those who are engaged in trade are making exhorbitant sums of money but are paying their workers minimum wages, then it is obviously not fair. Second, international free trade should not block new entrants from entering the market and competing. But if multinational giants are blocking the entries of small new companies, then the trade may not be fair. Finally, because of their relative economic power or lack thereof, partners in trade should not be short-changed. If partners in country A are getting much benefit and partners in country B are not, then the trade is not fair. In all of these cases, trade may be free, but if it is not fair, then the outcome of trade will be less than desirable. Free and fair trade must benefit all the parties participating. When all of the parties engaged in trade benefit, then consumers of both sides also benefit. As consumers receive the benefits of having more choice, good quality and cheaper products and services, there would also be better jobs created due to free and fair trade rather than just the opposite.

CONSUMERS NEED BETTER JOBS

In this book, the author has alluded to the fact that good jobs are essential for consumers to improve their income level and expand the economic base of the society. As major manufacturing firms continue to relocate outside the country, they are taking high-paying jobs along with them. Thus, ecologically responsible programs must be balanced with infrastructure development. Free and fair trade combined with environmental responsibility and infrastructure development must lead in the direction of creating and maintaining good jobs so that the economy can grow faster and more equitably.

Without such basic conceptual thinking, the American consumer cannot be empowered. All attempts to empower the consumer in the absence of a healthy environment, well-functioning infrastructure and well-paying jobs are likely to fail. Empowerment of the consumer, therefore, must have a certain positive direction. Consumers need better jobs and more access to economic and political decisions. Knowing full well that consumers have no control over the environmental behavior of the corporate entity, infrastructure development of the government and freedom as well as fairness of trade, consumer empowerment criteria can be clearly established by outside powers. Once again, the joint effort of the public and private sectors desperately needed in these all-important endeavors.

SUMMARY

This chapter deals with conditions that are not within the control of consumers and yet are essential for their well-being and empowerment. First, we start with environmental responsibility, which is essential for the future of society. It is maintained that the costing out of products should be given more attention. Although all products create both private and public cost, our accounting profession concentrates on the private cost and pays no attention to public cost. Hence, many products that generate excessive public cost and therefore must not be produced reach the market and cause excessive environmental damage. Some measures of environmental friendliness must be used before the product is considered for production.

The infrastructure that is essential for a smooth-functioning, efficient private sector must be continuously updated. This would enhance private productivity as well as minimize possible environmental damage. Thus it is maintained that infrustructure is the link between the economy and ecology. If that link is used properly, then a national sustainable development strategy can be successfully implemented. Consumer empowerment in these areas is just about nil. Somehow the leaders in the industrial sector do not make decisions from the perspective of their being consumers also. There must be certain common denominators agreed upon by all political parties so that nobody can play politics with these special issues. This is the only way consumers can be empowered regarding the environment and the infrastructure.

Without such a solution, there will never be a possibility for the mighty American economy to live up to its potential. In time if consumer empowerment for the environment and the infrastructure is not implemented, American society will suffer dearly.

REFERENCES

Baker, Linda (1999). "Real Wealth," *E-Magazine*, May–June, 36–41.

Bleakley, Fred R. (1995). "Many Firms Press States For Concessions; Tax, Other Deals Sought to Head off Defections," *Wall Street Journal*, March 8, AZ.

Business Week (2000). "Don't Take Economic Growth for Granted," January 17, 118.

Charnovitz, Steve (1996). "Sustainable Development," *Journal of Commerce*, April 16, 7A.

Danley, John, R. (1995). *The Role of Modern Corporation in a Free Society.* New York: St. John's University.

Drucker, Peter F. (1999). *Management Challenges for the 21st Century.* New York: HarperBusiness.

Easterbrook, Gregg (1989). "Cleaning Up," *Newsweek*, July 24, 27–42.

Fuller, Donald A. (1999). *Sustainable Marketing.* Thousand Oaks: Sage Publications.

Hart, Stuart L. (1997). "Beyond Greening: Strategies for a Sustainable World," *Harvard Business Review*, January–February, 66–67.

Ishibashi, Asako (1996). *Nikkei Weekly*, July 15, 1731–33.

Mahon, John F. and Kelley, Patricia C. (1987). "Managing Toxic Wastes— After Bhopal and Sandoz," *Long Range Planning*, August, 50–59.

Office of Solid Waste and Emergency Response (1989). *Annual Report.* Washington, DC: Environmental Protection Agency, EPA/68-01-7259, November.

Robles, B. Sanchez (1998). "The Role of Infrastructure Investment in Development: Some Macroeconomic Considerations," *International Journal of Transport Economics*, June, 113–149.

Samli, A. Coskun (1998). "A Method for Assessing the Environmental Friendliness of Products," *Journal of Macromarketing*, Spring, 34–40.

Sarkis, Joseph and Rasheed, Abdul (1995). "Greening the Manufacturing Function," *Business Horizons*, September–October, 17–28.

Sheth, Jagdish and Parvatiyar, Atul (1995). "Ecological Imperatives and the Role of Marketing." In M. J. Polonsky and A. T. Mintu-Wunsall (Eds.), *Environmental Marketing Strategies, Practice, Theory, and Research.* New York: Haworth.

_____ **Chapter 12**

Creating Greater Consumer Value

Our discussion, thus far, has been primarily in the direction of leveling the playing field so that consumers will have equal opportunity to improve the economic quality of their lives. In order to achieve this, our discussion proceeded in the direction of protecting, informing and educating consumers, improving the income distribution, making sure the environment is not deteriorating, developing the infrastructure and, above all, maintaining competition. However, over and beyond these activities that are related to infrastructure and competition, companies can also generate consumer value and other corporate practices that would further improve the position of the consumer in our society. It is crucial that businesses understand and function in the direction of generating such value. Additional consumer value, by definition, translates into profits for the private sector and implies the presence of a broader economic base for the public sector to draw from so that business conditions can be further improved. Thus, consumer value generation is a dynamic phenomenon creating an upward spiral toward empowerment of consumers and overall improvement of the economy. This consumer value generation is the crux of the gentleness and kindness of the market that has been referred to throughout this book.

HOW CONSUMER VALUE IS GENERATED

Samli (1993) analyzes some outstanding performances by a number of well-known companies. He identifies the common thread among these companies as that they all try to serve their respective target markets with value marketing. Samli (1993) then presents a discussion of value marketing. In this chapter, this concept is expanded and presented as an additional effort to empower the American consumer.

All companies that are surviving in the marketplace, by definition, are creating consumer value, because if consumers did not buy their goods or services, these firms would not remain in existence for long. However, monopolists or oligopolists can, by definition, force the consumer to buy their products or services. In such cases maximum consumer value is not created because consumers are forced to buy certain things that are not consumers' first choice, but their options are limited. This does not necessarily imply that companies are optimizing their profit picture either. If, for instance, banks, because of their oligopolistic power, were to pay very nominal interest on checking or saving accounts, it does not mean their profit picture is optimized. Indeed, consumers, who would be likely to deposit their cash in the case of high interest payments, are keeping their cash more in their homes or on their person or, indeed, they are paying off their debts faster. In other words, as banks reduce the interest they pay to their depositors, the cash banks receive from consumers is going down. Therefore, while banks are cutting down their cost of doing business by cutting down the interest rates they pay, they are also cutting down their profit potential by not receiving as much cash as they would were they to pay high interest on checking and savings accounts.

As this example illustrates, if consumers are given better opportunities, greater rewards and more powerful incentives, they will be engaged in more buying and selling transactions with all businesses. They will buy more products and services, they will spend more money on entertainment and education, and they will have a better quality of life as they make businesses more profitable.

Therefore, it stands to reason that by catering to the best interest of their customers, businesses are actually taking care of their own needs and improving their profit picture. This is what this author considers true market orientation. In order to develop such a beneficial orientation, businesses must be managed not *by* a bottom line but *for* a bottom line.

Consider, for instance, the following:

1. A drugstore in a small southeastern town has a very popular lunch counter. One day it is closed. The manager stated that it did not yield profit. However, the manager never considered that the people who had lunch at the store also bought a variety of other things.

2. A major department store insists on having its credit card business be a major profit center. Its merchandise sales volume and its mark-up rate is much higher than its credit card business return. If the interest it charges were to be somewhat lower, it would sell quite a bit more merchandise.

3. A convenience store believes in charging the same percentage markup on all products it sells. Many of the items in the store would be purchased more frequently if they were priced slightly lower.

As can be seen in all three cases, just because profit goals of the firms are established up-front in very rigid manners, the firms end up making less money than what they would otherwise make. This is what I call managing *by* a bottom line rather than managing *for* a bottom line. In other words, if the firm was managed *by* a bottom line, it would emphasize cost cutting, downsizing and other measures, not necessarily what benefits its customers but its own profit picture only. However, if a firm were to be managed *for* a bottom line, then it would do the best it could for its customers. It would develop a very close relationship with them and exchange customer satisfaction for profit. This is how many American businesses still make money. However, many of these are falling victim to merger mania. If all American firms were to be truly customer-oriented, the whole society would be better off. Many marketing professionals, such as myself, consider such consumer value generation as the true marketing function in the society. This is called value marketing (Samli 1993).

VALUE MARKETING AT WORK

Value marketing is a critical consumer value generator. Successful businesses thrive on retaining loyal and satisfied customers. As economic and market conditions change, firms must cater more and more to these loyalty and satisfaction concepts, and thus would maintain their existence and would prosper (Samli 1993).

Some years ago, Band (1989) stated that customer satisfaction is a straight-forward philosophy. It basically means putting the customer first. He implied that this is more important than simply increasing productivity, strengthening distribution systems or driving for a larger market share. This author maintains that putting the customer first is not mutually exclusive with all the other activities mentioned here. But putting the customer first enhances the success of all of other activities.

Customer satisfaction is a challenge for the firm. But with it also comes the best profit possibilities. Thus, the customer satisfaction challenge and how the firm faces it generates some developments in the marketplace. Consumers express concern about at least seven key areas when they are dealing with companies or just trying to satisfy their own needs as consumers. These seven key areas create major consumer anxiety, and anxiety interferes with the creation of consumer value. Understanding these seven problem areas and catering to them will pave the way toward generating more consumer value. All things being the same, value marketing implies a kinder and gentler approach to consumer well-being. These seven problem areas are product and service versatility; uncertainty; time management; market fragmentation and customization; quality, design and service; responsiveness; and constant improvement through front-line personnel. Exhibit 12–1 presents these seven problem areas as the facilitating factors for the development of a value marketing plan. The factors are discussed below.

Product and Service Versatility

Consumers always have questions about existing products and services whether or not these products or services will perform according the consumers' needs. If some people have somewhat special needs, would existing products be able to take care of these needs? Whether or not the corporate sector has the approach of "one size fits all" or provides versatile, flexible and adjustable products and services makes a difference. Ability to produce the best product mix efficiently is the ultimate in productivity.

Uncertainty

As changes take place in the market at an accelerated pace, consumer uncertainty also increases. This uncertainty could relate to the product-service quality, the level of confidence in the firm's ability to satisfy its customers' needs with their products or services. Whether or not they, the consumers, are making a good decision by purchasing that product needs to be in the affirmative. Many similar uncertainty problems need to be eliminated before the desired consumer value can be generated. By paying more

Exhibit 12-1
Consumer Anxiety and Parameters For Value Marketing Plans

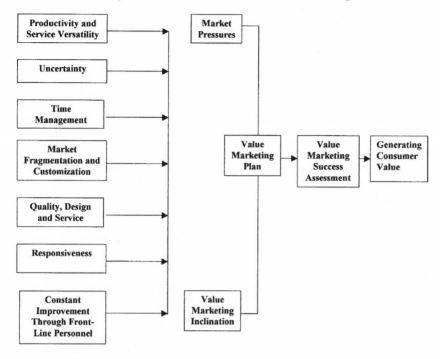

attention to consumer uncertainty and by trying to rectify it, firms can generate more consumer value and longer lasting relationships with their customers. Because customer needs and expectations change continuously, constant innovation of products and services is also necessary to adjust to these changes and to reduce uncertainty. Although research leading to innovations, initiating new ways of doing business and maintaining communications with markets may appear cost ineffective, at first sight, increased customer satisfaction through reduced uncertainty would more than offset this cost factor.

Time Management

In modern and unpredictable markets, time has become a competitive weapon. While changes occur in the marketplace, consumers are frustrated because there are always new and unexpected demands on their time. Those companies that can respond quickly, converting these changes to profitable solutions, manage to improve their competitive advantage. The firm, therefore, needs to be timely and must be able to bring new applications of technology to improve consumers' time-related anxiety.

Market Fragmentation and Customization

Consumers in today's markets are substantially better informed, more knowledgeable, more demanding and, perhaps above all, more changeable. Thus, markets are being defined and redefined constantly. New niche markets are discovered and, as a result, they are more and more fragmented. This fragmentation, subsequently, leads to market customization whereby each consumer receives different treatment according to his or her needs. Many major industries such as hospitals, travel, food and cosmetics have been cognizant of the emerging diversities in their markets. Hence, they have been attempting to customize their products or services accordingly. For the hospitality industry, for instance, innovations such as nonsmoking floors and specially located rooms for businesswomen who are traveling alone, availability of computers and other office-related equipment, along with exercise facilities and frequent customer programs are all part of the customization efforts of the industry that responds to diversities or fragmentation in its markets. Such customization is yielding better profits as it simultaneously generates more consumer value.

Quality, Design and Service

Those businesses that are being pressured to add more value to their products or services are making attempts to generate better quality, more innovative design and more value-adding services. Those companies that are succeeding in these endeavors are making more money and eliminating consumer anxiety. In some cases, unfortunately, it is not quite clear if companies are really attempting to improve the quality, design and service or simply are just talking about it. The "quality is job one" campaign of Ford Motor Company poses a question. The fact that Ford Motor Company has been rather successful in recent years may indicate that the campaign is taken quite seriously by consumers. Similarly, Toyota advertises the "Toyota Touch." These are quality products, quality service and quality people who are for consumers. Toyota has backed this claim with a commitment to total customer satisfaction, by a toll-free number for questions, concerns or complaints (Band 1989).

Responsiveness

Oligopolistic firms, as stated earlier, are gigantic, inflexible, uncreative firms that are far removed from markets and consumers. As they emphasize cost-cutting, mergers, increasing market share and downsizing, they pay more attention to what the other oligopolists are doing than what consumers need or want. Because their decision-making mechanisms are far removed from their markets and customers, they lack the necessary sensitivity and responsiveness to consumer needs. However, in this cyber age, consumer needs and concerns are changing rapidly. Such lack of responsiveness is not likely to generate consumer value by eliminating consumer concerns. Thus, regardless of size, firms must be as responsive as they can be to the demands of their markets.

Improvement Through Front-Line Personnel

Front-line personnel in companies perform a very critical function because they are the closest to customers and the work process. They essentially establish the necessary relationship with consumers and play a critical role in keeping them happy. These front-line people also know much about how to increase customer satisfaction and how to evaluate customers' attitudes toward the firm. They can provide continuous opportunity for improvement if the administrative unit of the company is susceptible to such ideas. If the ideas of the front-line personnel are harnessed systematically and regularly, greater consumer value can be generated.

These seven problem areas can be handled by the modern corporate entity. Proper treatment of each problem area will give one more opportunity to generate a value marketing plan that is keyed to generating additional consumer value. As illustrated in Exhibit 12-1, market pressures lead to value marketing. Hence, a value marketing plan is developed and implemented. The degree of success of this plan would be seen in the changing market position and the profit picture of the firm. Generating consumer value for profit is one of the key ingredients of the consumer empowerment efforts. If all firms have examined their profit picture from such a consumer-value-generation perspective, as opposed to pushing, bullying or misleading consumers, the total American market will certainly become a kinder, gentler and more profitable arena to work in. It is therefore necessary to examine the characteristics of a value marketing plan that caters to the seven consumer concerns and generates more consumer value for profit.

CONSTRUCTING A VALUE MARKETING PLAN

Although, in some sense, any marketing is value marketing in that marketing always adds some value, optimizing the buyers' and sellers' as well as society's values, however, requires a major effort on the part of the firm.

If the firm is genuinely interested in generating consumer value for profit, an eight-point marketing plan must be constructed and successfully implemented. These eight points are segment and target carefully, develop new products wisely, advertise proactively, promote effectively, price equitably, use sales/management successfully, handle and distribute cost effectively, monitor and generate feed back objectively.

Segmentation

Traditionally, businesses have segmented their markets on the basis of demographic and psychographic profiles of current and prospective customers. Similar profiles are grouped and treated identically.

In value marketing, in addition to the traditional approaches, actual behavior patterns are used to identify customers. Then these customers are associated with certain specific addresses, and statistical models are used to determine the value of each address. Customers, hence, receive customized offers individually or in tightly identified niches. Mary Kay built a multimillion-dollar business selling to women at home parties by using a network of beauty consultants. The turnover of these consultants was extremely high. In 1986 the company started building a database of its customers. As the consultants supplied the names of customers, each client received a Personalized Beauty Analysis, which consisted of a questionnaire completed by customers about skin type and color, hair color, facial shape and makeup preferences. Upon the analysis of these data, each customer received a diagram illustrating recommendations. This database in the early 1990s contained 9.5 million names. Since 1989 the party-plan selling process has been supplemented by five catalog mailings per year. The system developed by Mary Kay Cosmetics provides customers image-enhancing communication to position the firm's products with those of competitors and maintains an ongoing relationship. This was one of the forerunners of database marketing that can create consumer value and yield more profit for the company simultaneously.

Developing New Products

New products in the traditional approach are driven by more research and development and technology. In such cases, the firm's production system has had more to say on new product decisions. Therefore, in many cases, new product divisions are somewhat isolated from the conditions and realities of the marketplace.

Value marketing emphasizes not only the development of new products and services that would reflect the most up-to-date technology and would enhance the firm's market position against its competitors, but also would generate optimal consumer value. In such cases, it is critical to emphasize that consumer needs, more than anything else, would dictate the new product development process (Blattberg & Daighton 1991).

Advertising

Traditionally, mass communications or advertising is designed for the target groups as a whole. It has been more supply-oriented, reflecting the advertiser's point of view. In essence, advertising has not been all that forward-looking and consumer-oriented.

In value marketing creation, advertising should be based on information needs of individual customers. Consumer-driven magazine binding makes it possible to insert special messages selectively into print advertising. Other modern methods of communications, such as the Internet, make it possible to individualize advertising so that a much tighter communication with individuals can be established.

Promotion

Promotional offers traditionally are inserted in newspapers or magazines or mailed indiscriminately to various homes. This indiscriminate mailing is based on geodemographics.

In value marketing, however, promotion is much more carefully tailored to individuals' past behavior and special needs indicated by such behavior. This promotion is based on the expected payoff from promoting directly to consumers. The message is delivered specifically to the individual, creating a much tighter communication process between the marketer and the customer.

Pricing

Traditionally, products are priced differently according to costs and market segments. These prices are further adjusted on the basis of market acceptance and consumer reaction.

However, in value marketing, pricing is more readily based on the knowledge of individuals, their consumption habits, their needs, their price sensitivity and their past behaviors. Prices are further adjusted to each individual's ability to pay, along with all of these individuals' value needs or value perceptions. In essence, value marketing emphasizes pricing for reaching out to consumer markets as far as possible.

Sales Management

Typically, customer data have been used for the salespeople's own needs. As a result, the data related to sales performance are also kept with the sales group.

In value marketing, this traditional approach is modified. There is still access to customer files by the sales group, but the data are housed at the top management level and are also used to fulfill organizational goals. Calling on customers is based on this information. Prospect databases are tied to call reports that not only would improve sales force performance but also help monitor the sales effort and control its performance. In other words, while the sales effort is made more prospective-customer friendly, it is also more carefully administered. With the development of the Internet some marketers are capable of sharpening their sales management attempts to establish two-way communication with prospective customers. These people manage to receive detail information.

Product Handling and Distribution

Although, traditionally, organizations have been dependent on intermediaries and direct selling capabilities through their own sales forces to reach customers, these intermediaries or sales forces have had the tendency to take over and be concerned more about their own benefits than consumer benefits. Modern warehousing, transportation and other logistics activities are all purely cost-driven. This excessive bottom-line orientation up front has kept companies from materializing their market potentials in terms of sales volume and market share. Value marketing, on the other hand, emphasizes direct linkage to the market and the consumer. While intermediaries join the effort, they do not take over. All transportation, logistics and other merchandise-handling activities are evaluated first in regard to the value added to the customer and second to the cost effectiveness in generating this value. Optimizing end-user satisfaction generates more consumer value and greater profits simultaneously.

Monitoring and Developing Feedback

Market share, sales volume and the profit picture always have been critical tools for monitoring overall performance. Periodic review, usually annual, is used for adjustments.

Value marketing advocates also use these traditional measures but maintain that they be supplemented with early signals in the market. Success in retaining current customers, attrition (if any), the cost of acquiring new customers and the degree of customer satisfaction and its variations are analyzed. In essence, the value of the existing customer base is monitored on an ongoing basis.

As can be seen, value marketing requires some significant attitude changes toward the marketing process and the consumer. Exhibit 12–2 displays the essence of the value marketing orientation.

Perhaps Nieman-Marcus, WaldenBooks, and Brooks Brothers illustrate what value marketing is about. All of these firms are, according to Gill (1991): "enticing customers to remain loyal by adding value to their credit cards or creating purchase incentives for a core consumer group (p. 39). These proactive marketing plans, which are providing end users with greater value, may take different shapes, but they are composed of numerous basic features. These features are presented in Exhibit 12–2. However, there are final touches to be put together in developing value marketing.

PUTTING IT TOGETHER

There are at least nine final touches that would make value marketing truly valuable: (1) offer products that perform, (2) give more than the consumer expects, (3) give guarantees, (4) add more value, (5) avoid unrealistic pricing, (6) give consumers the facts, (7) build relationships, (8) penetrate the market, (9) monitor, monitor, monitor. A brief discussion follows below. This section draws heavily from Samli (1992).

Exhibit 12–2
Constructing a Value Marketing Plan

- **Segment and target carefully**

- **Develop new products wisely**

- **Advertise proactively**

- **Promote effectively**

- **Price equitably**

- **Use sales management successfully**

- **Handle and distribute cost effectively**

- **Monitor and generate feedback objectively**

Offer Products That Perform

Of course, this concept also includes services. Certainly, performance levels and their ability to generate consumer value vary from product to product and from service to service. Since the product or service is a bundle of utilities (Kotler 1997), offering a product that performs implies satisfying customers' needs and providing customers with optimum quality. Because better performance means more satisfaction and since more satisfaction leads to customer loyalty, this is almost a given as a measure for the company to strengthen its market position.

The same considerations are applicable to services as well. The proactive philosophy here should not be "give them any color they want as long as it is black" or simply "satisfy the consumers' needs," but it should be "let's delight our customers." In order to delight the customer, the firm must offer a very good product or service mix.

Give More Than the Consumer Expects

Attempting to delight the consumer through a value marketing plan goes beyond offering a good product or service. There must be a plus factor that the consumer did not even think of receiving. These may be frequent buyer programs; gifts with purchase that are given directly at the point of purchase, or redeemed by mail; or contests, sweepstakes and other related concepts that give consumers a real chance to win something by mail. There are many other factors such as environmentally sound packaging, including air conditioning in a car's standard price, free special delivery and the like.

Give Guarantees

Offering an enhanced and comprehensive warranty and paying full refunds without delay are critical features of a value marketing plan. Again, such a plan aims at delighting customers and gaining their loyalty. These are not high-cost factors and can easily be much higher revenue factors. This orientation basically is investing in the future.

Add More Value

When product handling, transportation and logistics issues are discussed, many value-added functions are brought to the fore. As value-adding functions are performed, end users or consumers will benefit from the cost savings and value-generating activities of the whole process. Of course it is essential that the proceeds of these cost-saving and value-adding activities be fairly shared with consumers. Thus, a value marketing plan must be supported with value-adding logistics-related functions. These cost-saving and value-adding functions, together, can provide the firm's customers with the best value possible.

Avoid Unrealistic Pricing

Companies should not think in terms of profit per unit. Empowering the American consumer is substantially related to profits by volume. Charging premium prices may not be justified by the product. It may not even work, given the competitive posture of the firm. Furthermore, if pricing was intended to maximize the utilization of the firm's total productive capacity and, hence, optimize profits by selling the largest possible volume, not only will the firm receive handsome returns on investment, but customers will receive great benefits from buying reasonably priced products and contributing to more widespread employment. Depending upon the intensity of the nature of turbulence, the price must be adjusted in the direction of gaining and keeping customer loyalty.

Give Consumers the Facts

It is important that consumers have valuable information that will enable them to make important purchase decisions through advertising, promotion, labels, packaging brochures, the Internet and so on. These decisions will increase the value received by consumers and will empower them to make better choices and optimize their own satisfaction. Both today's sophisticated customer and today's confused consumer need help to improve their purchase decisions and to feel good about themselves. Therefore, they demand factual and detailed information about the products and services they are considering buying. Developing sharper and better functioning communication systems with consumers will, no doubt, benefit both parties.

Build Relationships

Relationships mean additional customer value that translates into repeat sales. It also means added customer loyalty (loyalty toward the product, brand or company). Good marketing means repeat sales, and repeat sales imply a stronger market position or competitive advantage. Any and all such devices as frequent buyer plans, 800 numbers for additional product information, mall perks and membership clubs can all help enhance product, brand and company loyalty.

Penetrate the Market

No matter how small or big the target market is, it is necessary for the firm to use its production and distribution facilities fully. Therefore, special efforts must be made to capitalize economies of scale, scope and speed. Not only the products that work but also the products that are wanted, needed and desired must get into the hands of those who really want, need and desire them the most. This process must take place speedily and efficiently. Effectiveness in distribution and logistics is at least as important as efficiency (Samli 1992). The increased effectiveness enhances the value generated and delivered by marketing. As long as there are excess capacities in production, distribution and logistics, the firm is in a more vulnerable position in terms of unexpected change in competition and markets. Furthermore, it certainly is suboptimizing its profit opportunities. The firm, therefore, must penetrate the market at the core of the market, but also those who are at the periphery of the market will receive these products and services. When there is more for everybody at a reasonable profit, the firm will optimize its profit picture as consumers optimize the value they receive.

Monitor, Monitor, Monitor

If customer satisfaction is the acid test of value marketing and if value marketing enhances consumer empowerment, then there must be a constant monitoring activity. Among other means of monitoring, a customer satisfaction audit (CSA) is necessary (Band 1989; Samli 1993).

Companies must systematically determine the strengths and weakness in their current strategies for delivering high levels of customer satisfaction to enhance their competitive advantage and strengthen their market position further.

The customer satisfaction audit is an invaluable database to enhance the effectiveness of value marketing. It can take many different forms and can be composed of different components. However, if it serves its purpose, it certainly can be a very powerful competitive tool.

SUMMARY

In empowering the American consumer, the firm can try a little harder to generate consumer value, which indeed enhances its profit picture as well. This whole process is coined "value marketing." The firm, above all, must realize that consumers in the marketplace have certain anxieties, and eliminating them is critical. Seven consumer anxiety areas are identified in this chapter: product and service versatility; uncertainty; time management; market fragmentation and customization; quality, design and service; responsiveness; and constant improvement through front-line personnel. Counteracting these anxieties calls for a value-marketing plan. There are at least eight principles in constructing a marketing plan: segment and target carefully, develop new products wisely, advertise proactively, promote effectively, price equitably, use sales management successfully, handle and distribute cost effectively, monitor and generate feedback objectively.

Finally, in putting the whole thing together, the company can follow nine additional features that enhance the impact of value marketing: offer products that perform, give more than the consumer expects, give guarantees, add more value, avoid unrealistic pricing, give consumers the facts, build relationships, penetrate the market and monitor, monitor, monitor.

REFERENCES

Band, William (1989). "Are You Ready for the Customer Satisfaction Challenges of 1995?" *Sales and Marketing Management in Canada*, December, 19–20.

Blattburg, Robert C. and Daighton, John (1991). "Interactive Marketing: Exploiting the Age of Addressability," *Sloan Management Review*, Fall, 5–14.

Direct (1990). "Mary Kay, Avon Augment Salesforces with Data Bases," September, 24.

Gill, Penny (1991). "Added Value," *Stores*, October, 39–40.

Kotler, Philip (1997). *Marketing Management*. Englewood Cliffs, NJ: Prentice-Hall.

Lee, Leila Davis, McCusker, Tom and Marks, Don (1991). "Datamation 100: AST Research Inc.; Texas Instruments Inc.; Price Waterhouse; Novell, Inc.; Packard Bell Electronics, Inc." *Datamation*, June 15, 99–106.

Levere, Jane L. (1992). "The Value of Added Value," *Incentive* (Part 2), May, 18–21.

Samli, A. Coskun (1993). *Counterturbulence Marketing*. Westport CT: Quorum Books.

Samli, A. Coskun (1992). *Social Responsibility in Marketing*. Westport, CT: Quorum Books.

_____ **Chapter 13**

Conclusions and Future Research

The debate about the role of the federal government probably will never stop. Critics of the government, primarily big businesses and the religious right who have much to gain from having a very small federal government that does nothing else but dwell upon national defense, claim that Washington thinks we are all fools (Gehr 1997). But the unfortunate part of the whole deal is that in the private sector, mainly very large businesses also think that way. Furthermore, they try to treat consumers that way and usually they get away with it by using lobbyists, political action committees, other campaign funding pressures and, above all, by becoming bigger than the federal government. It is not the size of government, it is not who has the upper hand, government or the private sector; it is the empowerment of consumers so that the total populace can have a better quality of life.

At the time of writing this book, MCI and Sprint have announced a merger. This will be "the greatest merger" of all times. The CEOs of both companies appeared on TV and discussed how this merger could cut costs and save money for both companies. The question is still critical and remains unanswered: just what would the real benefits be to consumers? Will all those savings be shared equitably with consumers? How much of those cost-cutting arrangements would show up on consumers' monthly telephone bills? If this merger limits competition further, would these two companies truly feel the pressure to share these savings with consumers? Finally, what would happen to those thousands who would lose their jobs, will they become hamburger flippers? Would the gains from this merger outstrip the losses to society because of newly created unemployment?

There are no clear-cut answers to these questions, but past experiences with oligopolies and recent experiences with market share and consumer satisfaction in Sweden (Anderson et al. 1994) indicate that large market shares may lead to lower customer satisfaction, because the firm may be overextending itself or using more muscles than good business to generate profits. If the quality is not there, customer satisfaction may also decline (Anderson et al. 1994). Perhaps the worst thing about the merger of MCI and Sprint, or any other attempt to merge or in general about the merger mania, is that consumer well-being does not enter into the negotiations. Always cost savings and increased efficiencies are mentioned in merger negotiations, but it is never articulated just how these savings or efficiencies will benefit the consumer. Indeed, it is maintained throughout this book that if there is less competition, then there will be lesser inclination on the part of oligopolists to share the benefits of mergers with American consumers.

WHAT IF CONSUMERS ARE NOT EMPOWERED

If consumers are not empowered, there must be a question raised: What good is capitalism? After all, in American society, capitalism is practiced through the market system. If the practice of capitalism is based on gigantic companies which do not particularly care for the consumers' well-being, and they help accumulate wealth and economic power in the hands of few, they could still do well in the short run even though they are suboptimizing their profit potential and endangering the future of our society.

Although one of the basic tenets of capitalism is that one will work harder for greater revenues, this premise breaks down at a certain level. Even though a person making $30,000 a year may work twice as hard for $60,000 a year, the same analogy will not hold true for someone who is making $200 million a year. Certainly, someone who is making $200 million a year will not work twice as hard to make $400 million a year. Instead of going for empowering the consumer to make more money, which may take much more work, a CEO could decide that buying out the competition to make the same amount of money would be most attractive. That way the CEO may even work less because there is no serious competition now.

Indeed, market orientation by the corporate entity is costly, hard work and risky. Harris and Piercy (1997) maintain that not market orientation but becoming market-led is the key, and that is costly. Here we may distinguish between market orientation and performance. The firm may be market-oriented, but if it is not market-led it may not truly consider consumer empowerment as one of the main goals. Operationalization of market orientation is also difficult, and there are risks. Additionally, having an environmentally responsible, or green, orientation is both costly and risky (Fuller 1999; Handfield et al. 1996). Considering the risks, costs, and inconveniences, it is not difficult to conclude that the *path of least resistance* will be taken by the industrial giants. Meaning that they will not touch these inconvenience-creating difficult areas unless they are forced to. And so, of course, if the federal government is smaller, so much the better, as there will be no interference with their attempts to buy out the competition and go against consumer empowerment. This is unkind, not so gentle and in the long run not very profitable. Unchecked markets can easily create market tyranny. Tyranny is not kind or gentle; nor is it profitable in the long-run.

Exhibit 13–1 (top row) illustrates the fact that large oligopolists can adopt one of two key orientations. As shown, competition orientation which ends in buying out the competition, can establish a market tyranny. Presence of a tyrant in the marketplace is reflected in consumers' not having alternative choices, ability to participate in the market, or not having an opportunity to have a "say so" in the quality and prices of products or services. Such situations would create a further dichotomy between the rich and the poor, leading perhaps to class struggles that have taken place in the history of tyranny.

CONSUMER EMPOWERMENT MEANS PROFIT FOR BUSINESS

Left alone in the marketplace, with no foreseeable pressures from the federal government and consumer groups, there will be no immediate tendency for the merged MCI and Sprint to share the benefits of any cost savings and management efficiency (perhaps some in economies of scale, scope and speed) with American consumers or stakeholders. The fact is that if they were to take more of a market orientation path rather than one of competition orientation, it certainly would be more beneficial to the company as well as society as a whole. The well-being of consumers would not even be a consideration. In order for gigantic firms to follow a market-oriented position, first there must be lean, mean and hungry managers who are not quite as well off as their counterparts who make millions of dollars a year. However, this is not at all the present situation. At present CEOs

Exhibit 13-1
Far-Reaching Impacts of Two Corporate Orientations

Competition Orientation	→	Merger and Acquisitions	→	Profit Suboptimization	→	Market Tyranny

| Market Orientation | → | Consumer Empowerment | → | Profit Optimization | → | Market Prosperity |

appear to be making so much money that they are not likely to be quite motivated to take major risks and make significant changes. Second, consumers must already be empowered and must put much pressure on the giants to be more kind, gentle and caring. Third, the federal government must enforce the now almost defunct antitrust laws and must monitor the behavior of these giants. None of these conditions are likely to become a key factor for the empowerment of consumers. As was discussed throughout this book, the key factor in consumer empowerment is the corporate entity's understanding that a kinder and gentler approach to the markets is a more profitable proposition. Without such an understanding we all stand to lose much in terms of economic well-being. Happy consumers create better markets for all businesses, and that spells profit.

RECIPROCITY IN ECONOMIC PROGRESS

Even though there may not be enough lean, mean and hungry executives, one must not discard the magnificent American market (see chapter 5 of this book). As was discussed earlier, being kinder and gentler to the country's consumers can become economically so attractive that companies may do that not because they really care for the consumer, but because they are attracted to still greater levels of profit. Here there is yet to be discovered reciprocity. If businesses learn to delight consumers, consumers, in return, can delight businesses. This scenario certainly is very attractive, not only for consumers and businesses, but for America as a whole. But a reasonable government must be able to set the tone for such a reciprocity.

As has been mentioned in numerous parts of this book, the American market functions in the manner of a double-entry accounting system. Assuming the presence of a reasonable amount of consumer empowerment, meaning that consumers have some power and reasonable levels of income, if businesses satisfy consumers' needs better, they also make much greater profits. Thus, caring for people's business is good business (Samli 1992).

If the markets are not derailed, empowerment of consumers in America can become a reality. Throughout the book, we touched upon this point of derailment. American markets are derailed because of unrealistic accumulation of economic power in the hands of a few, mainly because of mergers and acquisitions. It is this derailment that makes the Clinton economy so different from the Adam Smith economy. Certainly at this time, it is not possible to even imagine an economy such as the one envisioned by Adam Smith. Therefore, Adam Smith's prescription of "laissez-faire" is not quite workable. It is also questionable if, given the complexity and conditions of our economy, such a prescription is at all workable. However, similarly, it is rather difficult to see how the economy got so derailed that it has the current problems as discussed at the beginning of this book.

The derailment can be stopped if:

- Instead of merger mania, competition is enhanced.
- Consumers have full access to better education.
- Consumers have full protection against questionable market practices, discrimination and harmful products as well as services.
- Consumers are fully informed about, carefully protected against and well-educated about the availability of products and services as well as their value.
- Consumers can get well-paying jobs and can improve their current economic well-being by receiving additional training and skills.
- Businesses are environmentally concerned and they opt for sustainable growth for the economy.

We have discussed these issues throughout this book. If these conditions are met and if there were genuine interest in consumer well-being, which in a capitalistic market system should go without saying, the American market will stop being derailed and it will reach optimal levels of its potential that are rather spectacular. Once again, a kinder and gentler approach would yield economic benefits to all.

A MATTER OF MEANS AND ENDS

Society can generate wealth for everyone. Society can generate profit for all businesses that create value. It is not really a zero-sum game. With the tremendous capacity to grow and with its equally tremendous unused capacity, the American economy has opportunity for everyone. However, excessive greed—that is, worrying about how much one makes at the cost of all others—does not provide economic growth opportunities. The end must be shared by all. If everyone benefits, if all consumers can improve their economic well-being, all businesses, particularly those that are large, will also make a lot of money. Thus, the end is being market-oriented to provide the consumers with the best. Unfortunately, if corporations are using the means of aiming at competitors and trying to get rid of them or trying to take them over, then consumers, the majority of the populace, will be unhappy because the country as a whole will not benefit. The economy will not grow, and probabilities for class wars will be increased as in every revolutionary movement in the history of the modern world. Many, if not all, of the revolutions in the history of mankind have been based on intolerable discrepancies in the economic well-being of social classes.

In the first scenario of optimizing the overall economic performance of American markets, the end definitely will justify the means; and in the second scenario of just a few overgrown and overpowered establishments just thinking about their own well-being, the means of corporate warfare (not healthy competition) will never be justified by the ends for which they operate. Most positive societal needs will be satisfied by the empowerment of the American consumer. The means of reaching this empowerment will be justified by the end of great economic gains and profits for all and the generation of equally great consumer value for all.

THE END IS A PROGRESSING SOCIETY

At the writing of this book, America stands at the crossroads of progression or regression. Partisanship and dogmatic indoctrination are so high and they blur the picture so badly that the average consumer does not even understand just what is to be done. Dogmas such as "private is better," "government cannot accomplish anything," "we must all become the followers of one religion [they all say that], we must not think and act we must put our faith in the market system" gain much strength because of private and selfish interests. Inciting these dogmas, we can go on almost indefinitely—particularly, if the inciters are in charge of the media. However, if we were to expand John F. Kennedy's famous statement: "My fellow citizens, ask not what your country can do for you, ask what you can do for your country," into "don't ask what the market can do for you, but ask what we all can do for the market since we are all part of it," American society will capitalize its own potential. It will require a clear-cut cooperation between the public and private sectors and, above all, it will require that the consumer, the life blood of the magnificent American market capitalism, be *empowered*. Without such an orientation, it is quite likely that there will be hard times for all. Capitalism is not feeding the greed of a privileged few, nor is it just taking care of a few whose needs are satisfied first and foremost. Capitalism is creating consumer value for all, regardless of race, creed or economic status. Market capitalism is the only way our society can generate proportionate amounts of profit and consumer value simultaneously. This is absolutely a great opportunity at this time. Just by caring for the consumer, by being kinder and gentler and by considering the total societal well-being, American government and businesses can easily perform multiple miracles.

THE MEANS ARE MARKET FORCES AND BUSINESS PRACTICES

As we said earlier, the end is a progressing society; the means are market forces and business practices. Naturally these must be at a level playing field which, as mentioned, begins with empowering the American consumer. If competition in the marketplace remains intact, then businesses will be forced to use more ingenuity to satisfy their customers and improve their own ability to generate consumer value. This situation is depicted in the bottom row of Exhibit 13–1. If the market is derailed with excessive attention paid to eliminating competitors and competition, the end result will be tyranny. However, if an overall market orientation is pursued, then the end result will be prosperity for all.

A FUTURE RESEARCH AGENDA

All that has been discussed in this book cannot be achieved overnight. Perhaps this six-item futuristic research agenda will be very useful:

1. *Exploring the conditions of a balanced growth process.* Throughout the book, it is implied directly or indirectly that balanced growth is critical for a developed economy such as ours. Certainly many less developed countries can achieve economic growth through unbalanced growth (Denery and Denery 1973). In recent years, newly industrialized countries such as South Korea, Taiwan, Singapore and Hong Kong are true examples of unbalanced growth. However, it is maintained here that Nurkse's (1953) old theory of balanced development is more appropriate for the American economy. It is necessary, therefore, to explore which industries must be brought up to par and which ones should be further emphasized for growth so that a balanced growth situation can be experienced.

2. *Social indicators to indicate a lack of balance.* It is critical to determine if the economy is growing and, if so, which sectors and what levels of discrepancy exist among these growth rates? These are some of the questions that need to be answered. Accordingly, decisions can be made as to how much should be invested in which industries. But exploring such controversial areas requires the utmost objectivity. It must all be based on scientifically generated data rather than hearsay or media blitzes.

3. *Consumer confidence.* As it was discussed earlier, consumer confidence is

a critical factor in consumption patterns and continuity in consumption. Although there are such measures, quite a bit more can be done with them in terms of their far-reaching implications in the economy. It is necessary to determine the limits and causes of consumer confidence, and the point must be made that it is critical to enhance it.

4. *Competitiveness evaluation.* Although much has been said throughout the book as to maintaining levels of competition in different economic sectors, much needs to be done here in regard to determining just to what extent a proposed merger is likely to reduce the competition. And just what are the pluses and minuses of such a proposition? Finally, what are the optimal levels of competition?

5. *Indicators of derailment.* If consumer empowerment is likely to take place, it is critical that the economy not be derailed. Reducing competition, eliminating the federal government's efforts to renew and advance the infrastructure, privatizing education and making it more accessible only to those who can pay, allowing the deterioration of the environment and misuse of resources—are all derailment activity. It will take more to stop the derailment later and rectify the damage done. There must be multiple measures to determine if the economy is moving in the right direction.

6. *Measuring double-entry market accounting.* Throughout this book, we emphasized the fact that the market in actuality functions like a double-entry accounting system. As consumers are empowered and competition is maintained on a level playing field, increased consumer value translates into profit. However, this is not totally automatic. If consumer value far exceeds profits, this situation may lead in the direction of inflation, and if profits were to far exceed consumer value generation, then the situation may go in the direction of a recession or a depression. Much research is needed to determine the balance between the two.

SUMMARY

This final chapter attempts to bring the basic premise of this book together: a kinder and gentler market is also more profitable market. It first raises the question: If consumers are not empowered, what good is capitalism? Then it argues that empowering the consumer is profitable business. But the market should not be derailed. If it does not get derailed, the market functions just like a double-entry accounting system. While consumer value is increasing, the level of profit is also rising. The whole society must work in this direction. That is putting the economic well-being of society ahead of party politics and other dogmatic stances.

Finally, the chapter proposes a research agenda that is likely to help improve society's chances to optimize its economic performance for all. Nobody needs to be left behind.

All in all there is a major philosophical message throughout the book and in this chapter: instead of letting the present form the future haphazardly, we must try to form the present based on key future goals. This is everybody's business. We must all be involved in it.

REFERENCES

Anderson, Eugene W., Fornell, Claes, and Lehmann, Donal R. (1994). "Customer Satisfaction, Market Share and Profitability," *Journal of Marketing*, October, 53–67.

Denery, David and Denery Lionel, (1973). "Cross Section Evidence for Balanced and Unbalanced Growth," *Review of Economies and Statistics*, November, 459–464.

Fuller, Donald A. (1999). *Sustainable Marketing*. Thousand Oaks: Sage Publications.

Gehr, Evan (1997). "Yes, Washington Thinks We're All Fools," *Wall Street Journal*, January 8, 18.

Handfield, Robert B., Walton, Steve V., Seegers, Lisa K., and Melnyk, Steven A. (1996). "Green Value Chain Practices in the Furniture Industry," *Journal of Operations Management*, November, 293–316.

Harris, Lloyd C., and Piercy, Nigel F. (1997). "Market Orientation is Free: The Real Cost of Becoming Market Led," *Management Decision*, January–February, 33–39.

Nurkse, R. (1953). *Problems of Capital Formation in Underdeveloped Countries*. Oxford: Oxford University Press.

Samli, A. Coskun (1992). *Social Responsibility in Marketing*. Westport, CT: Quorum Books.

Selected Bibliography

Barron, Kelly, and Marsh, Ann. 1998. "The Skills Gap: Why Do We Have
     a Worker Shortage in a Society with Considerable Residual Unem-
     ployment?" *Forbes*, February 23, 44–46.
Blanchard, Ken; Carlos, John P.; and Randolph, Alan. 1996. *Empowerment
     Takes More Than a Minute*. San Francisco: Berrett-Koehler Publish-
     ers.
Business Week, 1993. "The New Federalism: Tonic For World Growth,"
     June 7, 122–123.
Blattburg, Robert C., and Daighton, John. 1991. "Interactive Marketing:
     Exploiting the Age of Addressability," *Sloan Management Review*, Fall,
     5–14.
Drucker, Peter F. 1992. *Managing for the Future*. New York: Truman Talley
     Books.
Drucker, Peter F. 1999. "Beyond the Information Revolution," *The Atlantic
     Monthly*, October, 47–57.
Dugger, William M. 1989. "Instituted Process and Enabling Myth: The
     Two Faces of the Market," *Journal of Economic Issues*, June, 607–615.
Finley, Laurence. 1990. *Entrepreneurial Strategies*. Boston: PWS-Kent Pub-
     lishing Company.
Fuller, Donald A. 1999. *Sustainable Marketing*. Thousand Oaks: Sage Pub-
     lications.

Galbraith, J. Kenneth. 1967. *The New Industrial State*. Boston: Houghton Mifflin.

Gaski, John F. 1985. "Dangerous Territory: The Social Marketing Concept Revisited," *Business Horizons*, July/August, 42–47.

Griffin, Jennifer J. and Mahon, John F. 1997. "The Corporate Social Performance and Corporate Financial Performance Debate: Twenty-five Years of Incomparable Research," *Business and Society*, March, 5–32.

Hamel, G. and Prahalad, C. K. 1994. *Competing for the Future*. Boston: Harvard Business School Press.

Kelly, Kevin and Melcher, Richard A. 1995. "Power to the States," *Business Week*, August 7, 48–56.

Kennedy, John F. 1993. "Consumer Advisory Council: First Report." Executive Office of the President. Washington, DC: U.S. Government Printing Office, October.

Kotler, Philip; Jatusripitak, Somkid; and Maesincee, Suvit. 1997. *The Marketing of Nations*, New York: The Free Press.

Lardner, James. 1998. "A New Health Hazard: Economic Inequality," *The Washington Post National Weekly Edition*, August 24, 44.

Leonhardt, David. 1997. "Two-Tier Marketing," *Business Week*, March 17, 82–90.

Marino, Sal. 1997. "From Merger Mania to Spinoff Schizophrenia," *Industry Week*, January 20, 30–31.

Mark, Kenneth D. 1993. "Did Deregulation Affect Aircraft Engine Maintenance? An Empirical Policy Analysis," *Rand Journal of Economics*, Winter, 542–551.

Moore, James F. 1996. *The Death of Competition*, New York: HarperCollins.

Morgan, Neil A. and Piercy, Nigel F. 1996. "Competitive Advantage, Quality Strategy and the Role of Marketing," *British Journal of Management*, 7, 231–245.

Nelson, Bob. 1997. "The Care of Un-downsized," *Training and Development*, 51, April, 40–44.

Nurkse, R. 1953. *Problems of Capital Formation in Underdeveloped Countries*. Oxford: Oxford University Press.

Porter, Michael. 1990. *The Competitive Advantage of Nations*. New York: The Free Press.

Reingold, Jennifer and Grover, Ronald. 1999. "Is Greed Good?" *Business Week*, April 19, 85–99.

Ricardo, David. 1817. *On the Principles of Political Economy and Taxation*. London.

Robinson, Alan G. and Schroeder, Dean M. 1993. "Training Continuous Improvement and Human Relations," *California Management Review*, Winter, 35–58.

Samli, A. Coskun. 1992. *Social Responsibility in Marketing*. Westport, CT: Quorum Books.

Samli, A. Coskun. 1993. *Counterturbulence Marketing*, Westport, CT: Quorum Books.

Samli, A. Coskun. 1998. "A Method for Assessing the Environmental Friendliness of Products," *Journal of Macromarketing*, Spring, 34–40.

Samli, A. Coskun and Jacobs, Laurence. 1995. "Achieving Congruence Between Macro and Micro Generic Strategies: A Framework to Create International Competitive Advantage," *Journal of Macromarketing*, Fall, 23–32.

Scott, Bruce R. and Lodge, George. 1985. *U.S. Competitiveness in the World Economy*. Boston: Harvard Business School Press.

Sheth, Jagdish and Eshagi, Abdolreza. 1989. *Global Marketing Perspectives*. Cincinnati: Southwestern Publishing.

Sheth, Jagdish and Parvatiyar, Atul. 1995. "Ecological Imperatives and the Role of Marketing." In M. J. Polonsky and A. T. Mintu-Wunsall (eds.), *Environmental Marketing Strategies, Practice, Theory, and Research*. New York: Haworth.

"Sizing Up the Merger Mania." 1997. *Management Review*, December, 37–42.

Thurow, Lester. 1992. *Head to Head*. New York: William Morrow.

Thurow, Lester. 1996. *The Future of Capitalism*. New York: Penguin Books.

Walker, David B. 1996. "The Advent of an Ambiguous Federalism and the Emergence of New Federalism," *Public Administration Review*, May-June, 271–280.

Wieman, Clark. 1993. "Road Work Ahead: How to Solve the Infrastructure Crisis," *Technology Review*, January, 42–49.

Wills, James; Samli, A. Coskun; and Jacobs, Laurence. 1991. "Developing Global Products and Marketing Strategies," *Journal of Academy of Marketing Science*, Winter, 1–10.

Index

About the Author

A. COSKUN SAMLI is Research Professor of Marketing and International Business at the University of North Florida, Jacksonville. Author or coauthor of more than 250 scholarly articles, 12 books, and 30 monographs, he has been invited as a distinguished scholar to deliver papers at more than a dozen universities. He has lectured in countries around the world, is active in the Fulbright Commission, serves on the review boards of seven major journals, and is a Senior Fellow in the Academy of Marketing Science. Among his more recent books published by Quorum are: *Counterturbulence Marketing: A Proactive Strategy for Volatile Economic Times* (1993), *International Consumer Behavior: Its Impact on Marketing Strategy* (1995), *Information-Driven Marketing Decisions: Development of Strategic Information Systems* (1996), *and Strategic Marketing for Success in Retailing* (1998).